First published in Great Britain in 2021
by Cecil Lowry

ISBN: 978-1-910044-37-7

Website: cecillowry.wordpress.com

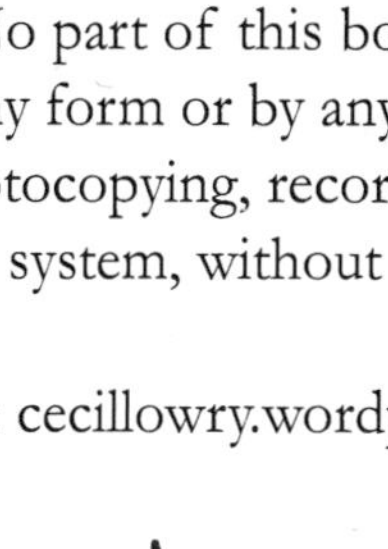

CONTENTS

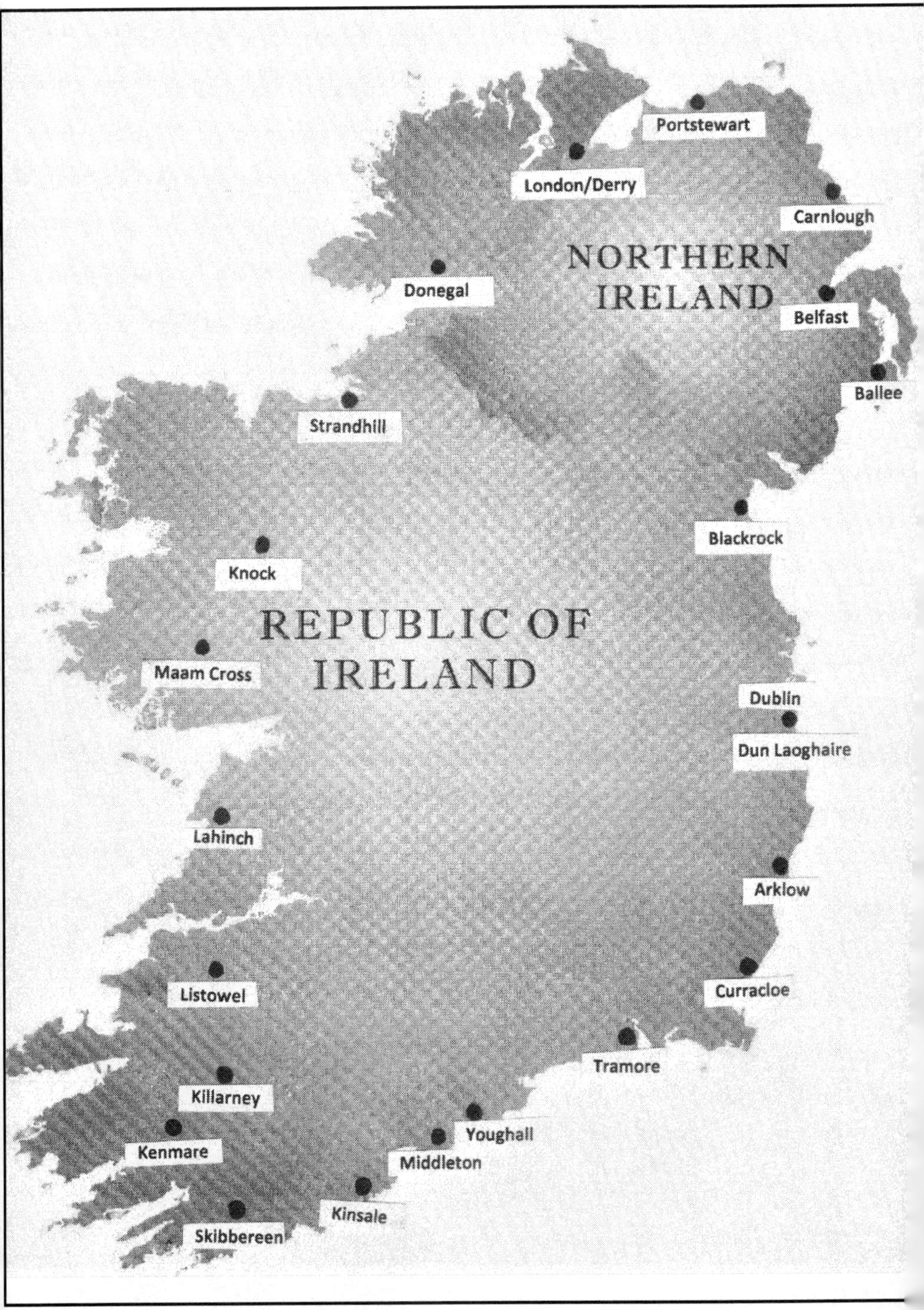

Portstewart
London/Derry
Carnlough
NORTHERN IRELAND
Donegal
Belfast
Ballee
Strandhill
Blackrock
Knock
REPUBLIC OF IRELAND
Maam Cross
Dublin
Dun Laoghaire
Lahinch
Arklow
Listowel
Curracloe
Tramore
Killarney
Youghall
Kenmare
Middleton
Kinsale
Skibbereen

Prologue

Ireland, Ireland: the words fall on the ear with the gentle persistence of rain on the shores of Kerry.

Honor Tracy in *Mind You, I've Said Nothing* (1953)

An old family friend once said to me: 'if you want to know about something, write a book about it.' That comment has stuck in my mind for a number of years - so this is my offering.

On a road bike, every turn of the wheels takes you about seven feet, around 750 revolutions per mile. My basic maths tells me that after hopefully covering more than 1,000 miles, I will have turned over the pedals around 1.3 million times during my trip, it's scary thought.

I must point out dear reader, before you jump on my crossbar, that I made this trip around the country of my birth in 2002. Cycling around the Island I kept a detailed diary and took quite a few photographs, albeit of dubious quality. Often, I would perch my little Nikon camera on a fence or a rock and dash back to get in some sort of position for a decent shot - apologies for the quality of some of them.

When I made my trip, the Republic of Ireland whilst in the EU, had not adopted the Euro and the currency was the Irish pound, known at the Punt, and border controls were still in force (to a degree anyway as you will find out later).

Any book about Ireland is sure to come with a warning, as Honor Tracy has already spelt out the pitfalls of writing about the country in her excellent book Mind You, I've Said Nothing, when she said about Ireland:

> *Any book on the burning subject then, even by an ignorant alien, is sure of eager perusers who will read it from cover to cover in an ecstasy of contradiction and pass an enjoyable hour or so listing the errors of fact, faults of grammar, misprints, foolish opinions, and other evidences of incapacity on the part of*

the writer, printer and publisher. Is writing about Ireland so risky an enterprise? Does it really require, if not the courage of a lion, at least the hide of a rhinoceros?

My only defence is that I'm not an alien – ignorant perhaps, and whilst I may have the courage of Lion, I certainly don't have the hide of a Rhinoceros.

As we cycle together along the highways and byways of the Emerald Isle, hopping from city to town to village, we will take time here and there to muse on the stories, the myths and the legends so prevalent in Ireland. We will encounter no end of tellers of tall stories and tales along the way, be they on the street corners, in the guest houses or propping up the bar in a local pub. I will introduce you to the average Irish person in a country where eccentricity is the norm. The writer's job is to observe and not to anticipate, and I hope this book reflects that. I have to be honest though and say that I did anticipate my pint of the black stuff at the end of each day.

I make no apologies for any errors of fact, faults of grammar, misprints, foolish opinions and other evidence of incapacity on my part, dear reader, but I hope that I can at least give you some idea of what it is like to cycle around the country of my birth.

Ireland lies at the most western point of Europe, a location not lost on the Romans as they never invaded the island. During the dark ages, when the rest of Europe was stumbling along in ignorance, Ireland was booming as a centre for civilisation and learning as Saints and scholars spread their wisdom. It was a moody and mischievous country, often misunderstood. Nothing in Ireland is straightforward, most names have two or three different spellings along with a plethora of pronunciations. Stories usually have different endings and legends different settings.

There is estimated to be around one million Irish-born people living outside of the country today, with another eight million still living there. If you are one of the nine million, or indeed anyone with an interest, then I'm sure you will find enjoy this book as we journey together round my beloved Ireland.

A combination of relief, elation and satisfaction engulfed me when I approached the large sign on the N11 a mile or so north of Dun Laoghaire.

'Baile Atha Cliath Welcome to Dublin' it proclaimed boldly. For the first time in twenty-two days, I lifted both hands from the handlebars, raised them above my head in a Tour de France salute, punched the sky in sheer exuberance and shouted 'I did it' at the top of my voice, oblivious to the stares of the locals passing by.

I had circumnavigated this most beautiful and historic island that has been inhabited by man since 6000 BC, on my own. I had cycled 1,000 miles and the sense of achievement was immense.

Travelling on a bicycle is undoubtedly the best possible way to see a country. Walking is too slow and travelling by car, train, bus or plane is too fast, but on a bicycle, you travel at just about a perfect speed for taking in the sights, unless of course the rain is hammering into your face, or the wind is so strong that your eyes never leave the tarmac – more about that later.

Jump into the saddle with me for a trip of a lifetime around the Emerald Isle. I hope you will find this a memorable book full of Irish reflection and wonder and that of course you will be encouraged to follow in my footsteps – sorry wheels.

Chapter 1

My Early Years

Born in the small town of Downpatrick, twenty miles south of Belfast in the province of Ulster, much of my early life was spent outdoors. I think I learnt to ride a bicycle when I was about five, and one of my earliest memories is of trundling around the pavements outside our home on a small tricycle. It must have been in the winter as the big coat and long socks might indicate – no gloves though.

I progressed from the three-wheeler to one of those sleek black Raleigh numbers with the revolutionary new Sturmey Archer gears, probably around my eighth birthday. I wanted one of those sleek racers with droopy handlebars, Derailleur gears and wafer-thin tyres, but my parents felt that the solidly built and reliable Raleigh was the better bike for me at that time (I never did get one of those racers, by the way, but there is still hope).

My childhood during the 1950s and early 60s growing up in the shadow of the Mourne Mountains and near the shores of the UK's largest inland waterway Strangford Lough (more about the lough later) was idyllic. Looking back however, what I didn't know at the time was how lucky I was to live in a rural farming community where food was plentiful and family connexions meant a lot. The people of Downpatrick looked after each other, regardless of their religious or political persuasions.

During the school holidays, my parents would sometimes take me on the odd trip across the border with the Republic of Ireland into the 'free State' as my dad called it. Whilst my dad termed it a 'good day out,' the main reason always seemed to be a shopping trip for the 'duty frees.'

At the south-eastern tip of county Down, Carlingford Lough marks the border between Northern Ireland and the Republic of Ireland. During the 1950s enterprising boatmen ran trips across the Lough from Warrenpoint to Omeath in County Louth. It was a journey of about an hour in our old Wolsey 1500 from Downpatrick to Warrenpoint and my dad knew that we had to join the queue early, in order to get a good seat in the bow of the boat. The diesel engine, usually situated in the mid-section, churned out noxious fumes engulfing those who had the misfortune to be sat near the stern.

During the 1950s luxury goods in the 'free state' were always cheaper than in the north and we always seemed to come home loaded up with cigarettes, lighters, watches and sundry other items. I'm sure my dad sold things on the black market, but as a nine-year-old I was not party to such things, but I guess it must have helped with the ice creams and sweets.

The trip across Carlingford Lough from Warrenpoint to Omeath is wonderfully summed up by Stephen Rynne in his Book All Ireland written in 1956, just about the time when I made my first trip across the Lough.

> *It is mid-afternoon and Omeath is a fever of excitement. Ferryboats are bringing people from the other side. The waterfront is thronged; everyone is in the highest good spirits. Is it because cigarettes are so many pence cheaper here than across the water? Or is it the sensation of being in the land of the free?*
>
> *Stephen Rynne - All Ireland*

Just over 100 years ago in May 1921, Ireland was partitioned by the British Government. The Anglo-Irish Treaty was signed six months later on 6 December, ending British rule in three out of the four provinces - well three and a quarter. The Irish Free State was created as a self-governing dominion with Northern Ireland remaining within the United Kingdom. It's not technically correct when I say three out of the four provinces, as Ulster is made up of nine counties of which three are in the Republic of Ireland and six in Northern Ireland. The counties of Donegal, Cavan and Monaghan, along with Down, Armagh, Fermanagh, Derry and Tyrone are in Ulster.

Many words have been used since 1922 to describe the two parts of the Island of Ireland, names such as – British occupied Ireland, the six counties, Ulster, the North or Northern Ireland, Eire, The Republic, the Free State or simply the South – so take your pick. For me it's simple, the Republic of Ireland will always be the south and Northern Ireland will always be the north.

When my school days drew to a close in June 1966, I became even more confused about my identity. Was I Irish, was I British, or indeed could I be both? My mother and father did nothing to clarify the situation for me as they were Church of Ireland protestants, but celebrated St Patrick's Day and all things Irish. Later in life, whilst researching my family history, I discover that my grandmother on my mother's side had been a Catholic but 'turned' – to use an Ulster expression – when she married my grandfather.

This perplexing question was put out of my mind when at the age of eighteen, a big adventure was calling on the other side of the Irish Sea. I am often asked by friends why I decided to leave my beautiful homeland, but I was becoming very aware of the delicate sectarian situation in Ulster, and I struggled to understand why there was so much friction and animosity between the two divided communities. If I am honest, I still do.

Sport was an important part of my early life and in 1966, I set off to enter Sunderland College of Education to study to be a Physical Education Teacher. In Sunderland I met a lovely English girl, and my Irish homeland took a back seat, as a career and family began to dominate my life.

It was almost forty years later, not long after I retired, that whilst lazing on a beach in Spain, I happened to read Tony Hawke's excellent book Round Ireland With a Fridge, possibly one of the funniest books I have ever read. My wife and friends had to endure my sudden bursts of laughter as they tried to doze on their sunbeds. Later that evening over a few glasses of sangria, they quizzed me as to why I had been guffawing earlier in the afternoon. After giving them a brief outline about Hawke's exploits, I foolishly blurted out: 'I think I might cycle right round the coast of Ireland.'

'Have you any idea how far that is'? They all chorused.

'I reckon it might be about 1,500 miles' I replied. 'I could probably do that in about fifteen days.' Cue great laughter. At that point in the evening, buoyed by a half litre of Sangria on a Spanish patio, I was determined that I would cycle around my native Ireland.

Chapter 2

Preparations

The first decision I had to make was when to attempt the trip. Late June would seem to be the best time, as statistically June is the driest month in Ireland and cycling in the rain has never been particularly attractive to me. Statistics of course, are all well and good, but Ireland is not called the Emerald Isle for nothing, so a guarantee of dry weather at any time of the year should always be taken with a pinch of salt. This logic was reinforced when I read Bulfin's book, Rambles in Eirinn. He started his journey on the last day of June and wrote:

> *'the weather was perfect, in fact it was hot, or as the locals said to him at the time 'it is shocking warm' and 'scorching', 'and terrible hot, glory be to God'.*

Another reason to choose June is that the peak holiday season in Ireland does not start until early July, so the B&Bs and guest houses should usually have vacancies. With daily mileage uncertain, there would be little point in me booking accommodation in advance so I will just have to take potluck on availability at the end of each day.

It was a cold December evening when I settled down in my study over a glass of wine and a faded map of Ireland to plan the trip. Out came the coloured felt tip pens, and very soon any thought of cycling round the entire coastline of the country was quickly abandoned when I discovered that it would be more than 3,000 miles. At an average of fifty miles a day, that would take me almost two months. A journey of around 1,000 miles seemed more realistic, sticking to the coastline where possible and avoiding as many of the larger towns and cities.

Before finalising the route, my first decision was to decide which way round the island to travel. Should I go clockwise or anti-clockwise? After wrestling with this dilemma for sixty seconds, I decided to apply a scientific theory and toss a coin. Heads clockwise, tails anti-clockwise. It fell tails so it's anti-clockwise.

My next decision was to decide if my bicycle would be up to the challenge. As a five-year-old hybrid and in reasonable condition, I was confident that it would see me through the trip and avoid the expense of buying a newer model. The saddle was not very comfortable, and as it was to be my 'closest' friend for three weeks, I decided to buy a new one.

'Saddles are very individual things, but I would recommend the Selle Italia model,' said the manager of my local cycle shop, producing a sleek but hard looking little number.

'You don't want a saddle with too much padding as the movement can cause friction, and you also need a decent waterproof pair of panniers to carry all your kit,' hc added.

He goes on to tell me that weight is critical for a long-distance cyclist, and I don't mean my own body weight, but the weight of the 'necessary' items that I intend to carry with me.

'You don't want to be carrying the equivalent of a couple of bags of potatoes in your panniers' he adds. Very apt as I am heading for the spiritual home of the spud. He recommended a shiny pair of blue panniers: 'They're totally waterproof as it's important on such a long trip that you keep your clothes dry.

'What about cleats?' he added, as we went through the various items that I might need.

'All the top cyclists use them, they're like ski bindings that enable you to clip your shoes into the pedals as they can considerably reduce the effort you need to apply to the pedals. With normal shoes you can only apply effort on the downward movement of each leg, whilst the other leg simply drifts freely upwards. With both feet clamped onto the pedals you can apply effort both up and down with both legs on each revolution.' Bowing to his expert advice, I purchased a pair of cleated pedals.

The next day and with my new Selle saddle firmly bolted on and my cleats in place, I set off on the first of my 'test rides' into the hills of the Peak District near where I live. It felt strange to have my feet locked into the pedals and the first time I braked to a stop I managed to topple over as I forgot that I had to twist at least one foot through ninety degrees before placing it on the ground. I was finding it difficult to get into a comfortable riding position on my new saddle and no matter how I twisted and squirmed my bum kept complaining. I was tempted to take the saddle back to the shop and revert to my old trusted and battered one, but I stuck with it and as the weeks went past, my 'cheeks' became accustomed to its contours, or maybe the contours of the saddle became accustomed to my cheeks, but it began to feel quite comfortable on a long ride.

During those long training runs in the hills around Buxton in the Peak District, I began to appreciate the enormity of the task ahead when I discovered that my worst enemy was not going to be cycling up the steep Irish hills, but the wind, and I don't mean the wind that comes because of the Guinness. As any cyclist will tell you, the wind is a fundamental part of life, with a weight, texture, energy, motion and moods all of its own. Cyclists have always classed the wind as the 'invisible hill' where your legs must produce eight times as much power. What have I let myself in for?

During my trip I got paranoid about the wind. When the weather forecast came on the radio each morning, I ignored the rain and prayed that there would not be too much wind. More later.

As 'I' day approached I stepped up my training but with just a couple of weeks to go, I still had not hit more than 50 miles in one day, let alone 50 miles a day for three weeks.

It was now early June, and with a matter of days until my trip, I began to pay more attention to the Irish weather forecasts. It's well known that there is no such thing as climate in Ireland, only rapidly changing weather patterns, but I religiously scanned the long-range forecasts, nonetheless.

The logical starting and finishing point for a cycle round Ireland should of course be its capital city Dublin and to get there it would be about a two-hour drive to Holyhead from my home in Stockport to the port of Anglesey from where ferries depart regularly for Dublin and Dun Laoghaire.

□

Chapter 3
Getting there

I spend the evening before 'I' day nervously packing my panniers with essential items and doing a last-minute check on the bike, leaving things out and then putting them back in again. Sleep proves difficult, but after a large glass of my dad's favourite tipple, Bushmills whiskey, I eventually drop off.

It's Sunday morning and the big day has now arrived. The reality of what I'm about to embark on, finally dawns on me. A mixture of excitement and fear kicks in over breakfast, what have I let myself in for?

Double checking my panniers, I load the bike on to the roof rack. 'This is it, no turning back now,' I say to Liz as we set off on the journey down the M56 towards North Wales.

The port town of Holyhead is busy on this Sunday morning in mid-June when we arrived at the ferry terminal. Leaving my wife Liz to look after the bike, I pop into the terminal building and produce my ticket at the Irish Ferries check-in desk. I have allowed myself at least a half an hour before the ferry is due to depart, but I'm stunned when the check in clerk tells me, 'Sorry sir but the ferry sailed 15 minutes ago, it had to leave its berth early due to an incoming ferry, but there's no problem, we have transferred you to the Stena Line ferry and it's due to leave in five minutes. Quick as you can, they are delaying departure for you,' she says calmly.

I run back to the car, rip the bike from its rack, clip on my panniers, quickly kiss my wife Liz goodbye and cycle up the car ramp onto the Stena Explorer. As I cycle into the vast cavernous interior of the ship, the crew raise the ramp behind me and help me secure the bike between a Volvo and a Mercedes.

Settling back into a comfortable seat in the ship's lounge and gazing out over the calm waters of the Irish sea, I realise that my great adventure has begun. That feeling of apprehension and excitement makes the hairs on the back of my neck tingle.

My booking with Irish Ferries would have taken me straight into Dublin port, but it suddenly dawns on me that the Stena Line ferries sail into the port of Dun Laoghaire (pronounced Dun Leery) some eight miles south of Dublin. An extra forty-five minutes of cycling on my first day is not a huge issue though in the big picture of 1,000 miles.

As the Stena Explorer ploughs across the 'snot green' Irish Sea (Joyce) and nears the Irish coastline, my heart begins to beat just that little bit faster. My first glimpse of the Emerald Isle is of the Wicklow Hills just to the south-west of Dublin. Approaching Dun Laoghaire, I gaze with some apprehension through the lounge windows at the island that is to test my mental and physical strength for the next three weeks.

As I mentioned earlier, one of the disadvantages of arriving in Dun Laoghaire rather than Dublin Port, is that I now need to get right through Dublin from south to north. I study my map and decide that I have two choices, I can cycle right through the busy city centre and down O'Connell Street or cross the Liffey via the Tom Clarke toll bridge near to the docks. It's tempting to cycle through Ireland's historic capital, but as I'm an hour behind schedule, the toll bridge option looks the best bet as I can head on north skirting around the east side of the city.

□

Chapter 4

Day 1 – Dublin to Blackrock (62 miles)

It's late morning when I cycle down the ramp onto Irish soil and into the province of Leinster. Leinster is one of the most densely populated of the four provinces, with the capital Dublin making up the vast majority of its population of around 1.2 million people.

One of the benefits of being on a bicycle is that you are rarely held up in traffic queues and I am waved straight past the queues of cars and lorries waiting to disembark. Gliding effortlessly along the smooth tarmac out of the ferry terminal, I'm soon on my way northwards.

The N31 hugs the south side of Dublin Bay with the DART (Dublin Area Rapid Transport) running alongside. The DART runs along the line of Ireland's first suburban commuter railway, opened between Dun Laoghaire and Dublin in 1834. The views across the Bay to the north are superb and it has often been described as a lookalike for the Bay of Naples.

At Blackrock the N31 turns inland, and I cycle on along the R118 towards the Liffey. Approaching the docks area, I cycle through one of Dublin's most notorious areas – Ringsend. Boarded up buildings and disused warehouses line the streets, and it feels quite intimidating even on a bright June morning.

John Gamble on visiting the Ringsend area in 1912 wrote:

> *Nothing can be more filthy and disgusting than the town of Ringsend at which the pier terminates. Ringsend … the most horrible stink of filth ever beheld.*

Cycling through Ringsend, I must keep my wits about me to avoid the cyclist's nightmare – broken glass – as the streets and pavements are covered with it.

Crossing the toll bridge over the River Liffey (fortunately free for cyclists), the sun lights up the city centre away to my left. Dublin in the sunshine is a city of colours and today it seems to exude vitality over a river that carves it in two like a slash with a felt tip pen. With its eleven bridges along a two-mile stretch, the Liffey provides a focal point for the many thousands of tourists who visit Ireland's capital each year, and although not one of the world's cleanest waterways, it has an attraction all its own. Perhaps the fact that it bears a striking resemblance to one of Ireland's favourite tipples may have something to do with it. During a visit to the brewery in 2011, Prince Philip joked as his pint was delicately poured: 'Is it made with Liffey water?'

It is well known that Dublin is synonymous with Guinness, or should we say that Guinness is synonymous with Dublin. Guinness served outside Ireland is usually somewhere from 'passable to passed water' (thanks to my friend Stephen Jones of the Sunday Times for this one). It was reported once that when a black Irish gentleman was asked what it was like to be black and Irish, he replied, 'like a pint of Guinness, of course.'

Leaving the Liffey behind I head for the N1, the main road out of Dublin to the north. It's Sunday lunchtime and whilst the roads are relatively traffic free, I need to keep my eyes open as vans and various other odd modes of transport leave the many churches and chapels in the area. Cycling along the R131 I pass Ireland's most famous sports stadium Croke Park, Ireland's premier Gaelic games stadium. The stadium has served as both the principal stadium and headquarters of the Gaelic Athletic Association (GAA) since 1891.

At Drumcondra I join the N1 and cycle on northwards, leaving the N1 at Whitehall and joining the R132 towards Swords and Dublin International Airport. At this point, the N1 becomes the M50 and of course cyclists are banned on motorways. The road climbs steadily before levelling out near another of Ireland's sporting stadiums, the Morton Athletics Stadium at Santry. The stadium was opened in 1958 with a cinder track and on 6 August that year, Australian Herb Elliott shattered the world record for the mile run with a time of three minutes fifty-four point five seconds. This was the first race in which five athletes had run a four-minute mile. The Morton stadium is also the home of League of Ireland Football Club, Shamrock Rovers. Considering it is now mid-June the sign outside the stadium reads: 'Next home match v Derry City – 6th January.'

A few miles later, I'm passing Dublin International Airport and making good progress towards Drogheda. Just after the airport I leave the R132 on the

Naul Road, past the Forrest Little Golf club and onto the R108. I knew that punctures would be inevitable on such a long trip, but it's really annoying to get one after cycling a mere eighteeen miles on day one. It takes me just a couple of minutes to replace the tube with well-rehearsed efficiency and I cycle on through the villages of Ballyboghil and Naul before crossing the River Delvin into County Meath – only fifteen more counties to go.

At this point I get my first experience of Irish road signs. As it is part of the EU, the Republic of Ireland's road signs are now in kilometres instead of miles, but of course they still haven't got around to replacing many of the older ones which still show distances in miles.

Half an hour's easy cycling later and I am coasting downhill into Drogheda, bidding farewell to Meath and crossing into my third County, Louth – three counties ticked off already on my first day.

Hugging a bend in the river Boyne as it wends its way towards the Irish Sea, the town of Drogheda sits at the coastal end of the river valley. Up to 911 Drogheda was a just a small hamlet, before it began to take shape as a major town when Hugh de Lacey, Lord of Meath developed it into an important Norman stronghold with a bustling port.

Drogheda's darkest years came in September 1649 when one thousand Irishmen and women were massacred over five days by Cromwell's forces in St Peter's Church. Since 1642, most of Ireland had been under the control of the Irish Catholic Confederation and with his New Model Army, Cromwell landed in Ireland to re-conquer the country on behalf of the English Parliament.

Having not eaten since leaving Dun Laoghaire, I stop for a few minutes to devour a delicious sandwich on the Bridge of Peace that crosses the river Boyne. Built as a part of an inner by-pass of the town in the 1970s, the bridge got its name when the troubles raged in Northern Ireland and a peace rally was held there in 1976. Using the symbolic River Boyne as a meeting point, more than 15,000 people marched on a bitter cold day calling for peace in Ireland.

Gazing eastwards along the river my thoughts wander back to the Battle of the Boyne in 1690, a year that is indelibly etched in my memory. One of the most well-known military conflicts in Irish history, the battle was fought a few miles upriver from where I'm standing on 12 July 1690. In a wooded valley, the Protestant King William, better known as William of Orange, defeated his father-in-law the Catholic King James II in a battle so significant that it shaped the future history of Ireland. An often-forgotten fact was that the Pope of the day supported William of Orange. This unusual alliance came about because the Papacy, then a world power, was at odds with King Louis XIV of France, who was an ally of King James. It is said that a Mass of deliverance was celebrated in Rome after King William's victory.

Leaving Drogheda, I press on along the R166 towards the small town of Togher, hitting the coast again a mile or so south of the quaint little seaside town of Annagassin on the south shore of Dundalk Bay.

It's now late afternoon, and with fifty-six miles on the clock, I'm looking forward to my first night's rest. Dundalk is a possible target for my first overnight stop, but on a whim, I decide to scrap that idea and head on east along the R172 towards the seaside village of Blackrock.

The Blackrock promenade is busy on a late Sunday afternoon when I arrive. Cars are parked nose to tail, and the seafront is crowded with people licking ice creams or eating sandwiches whilst gazing out over the calm blue waters of the bay, a practice that has been common on summer Sunday afternoons in Ireland for many years, as I well remember from my youth.

Cycling along Main Street, the first two houses with B&B signs outside have 'full' on them, perhaps I have made a mistake and may have to cycle the four miles to Dundalk. At the northern end of the town, I spot a B&B sign outside Blackrock House that has 'vacancies' on it and I breathe a sigh of relief.

The aptly named Blackrock House is owned by Gerry and Brenda and without even asking the price, I settle into a comfortable room with views across the bay and unpack my panniers. Sixty-two miles cycled on my first day around Ireland – not a bad start.

After a shower and a short nap, I remember the first rule for cyclists and travel writers: 'On arrival at your destination, buy a local paper and go for a drink in a pub.' The local paper anywhere in the world, will often tell you more about an area than any glossy guidebook, and a pub will give you an immediate feel for the town and its inhabitants.

Strolling along main street I pop into the Bayview Inn for my first, and most anticipated pint of the black stuff. It is still only 7pm but the Bayview is already busy with early drinkers (or perhaps late drinkers from a lunchtime session). Pints are flowing across the bar as if on a conveyor belt and the sound of Irish laughter reverberates around the lounge. I order my pint and wait the seemingly interminable time for it to be pulled. Having lived away for so long, I've forgotten that it takes a full three minutes to pull the perfect pint of Guinness.

There is very little chance of being lonely in an Irish pub and as I'm waiting for my first pint to settle, I strike up a conversation with a couple of the locals at the bar. Within a couple of minutes this conversation with two people turns into a group discussion as others join in. If you have been to an Irish pub, you will know that people tend to drift in and out of several different conversations. Suddenly the person you have been speaking to has turned away and is now holding a second conversation with someone further along the bar. If you have not been in an Irish pub, you may think it's a bit rude, but it's just part of the scene and the person will turn back to you a few minutes later and carry on with the original conversation.

Finding a quiet table in the corner, I take my first (but not my last) sip of the delicious black stuff and open the local paper, the Dundalk Argus. As with most local papers in Ireland the Argos is full of gossip interspersed with national news, with the back pages devoted to the traditional Irish sports of Gaelic Football, Hurling and Camogie, with a bit of Soccer and Rugby thrown in.

After a couple of pints in the Bayview I wander down the main street on the lookout for somewhere to eat. As most of the restaurants seem to be full, I settle for chicken and chips from a take-away just a few doors along from the pub.

Although it's been a long day and I'm very tired, I'm at peace with the world sitting eating my supper on a bench on the Blackrock Sea front, whilst gazing out across the Irish Sea. After popping the last chip into my mouth, I'm tempted to pop back into the Bayview for another pint, but I decide to call it a day and head back to the Bayview for an early night.

Undressing rather gingerly, the full impact of the first day's exertions hits me as I lie back on the bed. My thigh muscles have seized up and my shoulders are aching, but within seconds I drop off into a deep sleep.

Day's statistics: 61.6 miles – Average speed – 12.2mph – Time taken – 5hours 53 minutes – Max speed – 34.5mph

Chapter 5

Day 2 – Blackrock to Ballee (62 miles)

My muscles are as stiff as boards as I swing my legs out of bed in Blackrock House on the morning of day two – only another twenty days and 920 miles to go.

Brenda's full Irish breakfast is delicious, and I console myself with the thought that at least I have at least another twenty of these sumptuous fares to look forward to along with a few more delicious pints of the black stuff. I have no qualms about clearing my plate as I need the calories for my assault on the border into Northern Ireland.

After a few stretching exercises I make my first acquaintance with what is to become my daily morning ritual of 'vaselining' up. As every serious cyclist knows, Vaseline, or one of its many competitors is our lifesaver. Without spreading some of this gooey substance around your private parts, tit can become painful later in the day when your bum cheeks have been rubbing against lycra for hours on end.

It is a sunny windless Monday morning when I clip into my pedals, leave Blackrock House, and cycle along the deserted Blackrock seafront onto the R172.

Twenty minutes later and I'm cycling through Dundalk, the county town of Louth. Dundalk used to be at the northern extent of the English Pale during the 15th Century and is the last large town before the border with Northern Ireland. The Pale was the part of Ireland directly under the control of the English government in the Late Middle Ages. By the late 15th Century, it had been reduced to an area along the east coast stretching from near where I started my trip in Dun Laoghaire, to Dundalk.

I have about a 60-mile ride ahead of me today to reach my friends Derek and Francis McCann's farm near Downpatrick. This is my only 'must reach' destination for the trip as the local newspaper in Downpatrick, *The Down Recorder* has arranged to interview and photograph me on the morning of day three.

The most direct route will take me via the border town of Newry, but I decide to stick to the coastline and head for the small village of Omeath where a ferry used to run across Carlingford Lough to Warrenpoint. (a journey on a ferry that I mentioned earlier). I have no idea if this ferry still operates, but I decide to take the chance anyway and head north along the N52 before turning onto the R173 and head along the south coast of the bay towards Carlingford.

The R173 runs along the Cooley Peninsula, a chunky finger of land some twenty-five miles long that separates Carlingford Lough from Dundalk Bay. The views back towards Blackrock and Dunmany Point are spectacular but I can only take a few quick glances over my shoulder as a steady incline into a stiff headwind and lots of potholes, keeps my head down over the handlebars.

The Carlingford mountains rise imposingly to a height of 2,000 feet up to my left. These mountains are historically significant in that they formed the ancient frontier of Ulster when many a battle was fought between the English and the Irish in and around their steep slopes where warriors played their part in the age-old battle between the men of Ulster and Queen Maebh of Connaught.

The last mile or so into the picturesque town of Carlingford is downhill giving me the opportunity to enjoy the views across the Lough to Ulster lift my spirits – home is in sight.

Originally a small Viking settlement, Carlingford was invaded by the Norman knight Hugh de Lacy in the eleventh century when he laid the foundation stone for a castle on a strategic outcrop of rock. The castle is now known by the name of King John's Castle following a visit by him in the year 1210 and offers dazzling perspectives over the Lough towards the Mourne Mountains. Local legend has it that King John decided to stay here instead of Belfast for approximately three days that year.

With its secure and beautiful harbour at the foot of the mountains, the Normans developed Carlingford into a significant port. It was one of Ireland's major ports at that time. Eight centuries later it was overtaken by its near neighbour Greenore, just three miles to the east, before Dublin and

Dun Laoghaire took over that role in 1926. Carlingford today is mainly a fishing and pleasure port.

Pulling up outside the Carlingford tourist information office, I pop in to enquire if the ferry service across the Lough is still operating.

'Is there still a ferry running from Omeath to Warrenpoint? I'm cycling round Ireland and I need to get across to County Down,' I enquire.

'It only runs on a Sunday, sir,' replies the polite and friendly assistant.

Noticing the look of disappointment on my face she adds, 'there is a chap down in the harbour who takes tourists on trips out into the Lough, he might take you across, why don't you pop down and ask him.'

If I cannot get across the Lough, I will have to cycle an extra twelve miles into Newry and then another twelve back along the north shore to Greencastle, putting an extra twenty-four miles onto my day's cycle.

Thanking the nice assistant and with my fingers crossed, I cycle down onto the quayside where the skipper of the cruiser, is busy on deck.

'I understand you do pleasure cruises, any chance of taking me and my bike across the Lough to Greencastle'? I call down.

'Love to mate but the tide is on the ebb and if I get across, I'd not get back until next high tide which is late tonight. Bernard over there will be going back over shortly, he lives over in Greencastle, and he might give you a lift.'

He indicates across the quay where a 30-foot mussel fish boat, piled high with bags of mussels is being unloaded.

After a quick thank you to Peter, I cycle off to the other side of the quay.

Looking down onto the slick operation as the crew unload bags of mussels.

'Any chance of a life across the Lough?' I shout down to the two men working on the deck below.

'No problem mate, if you can wait for about half an hour or so until we unload the catch, we'll tak ye across,' one of the crew shouts.

'Thanks, much appreciated.' I reply.

Carlingford Lough's large populations of blue mussels and oysters are exported all over the world and much sought after. They are found in wild mussel beds and are farmed in aquaculture sites within the Lough.

Sitting on the harbour wall munching a chocolate bar, I watch what is obviously a well-practised procedure. Bags of mussels, each the size of a large bag of cement, are lifted from the boat by a hoist, stacked in a huge pile of probably forty or fifty and then wrapped around with what looks like a huge roll of cling film.

When the crew finish unloading the mussels, my bike is lowered down from the quayside on the mussel hoist where Bernard, who turns out to be the skipper, spreads out an old set of oilskins for me to sit on. The engine is started, and we set off for the forty-minute journey across Carlingford Lough.

As we chug our way towards Greencastle, I strike up a conversation with Bernard and his mate, Pat.

'We leave home before daybreak every day and are unloading our catch by noon. As the mussel season is relatively short, we work as jobbing builders for the rest of the year. It's a bit of a family thing in these parts, my father and grandfather were both mussel fishermen,' Bernard tells me.

As we approach Greencastle, I expect them to pull up alongside the small jetty, but they pick up a buoy where a dingy is tethered about one hundred metres from the jetty. My first thought is, 'how are the three of us, plus my bike, and gear going to get ashore without at least two trips in this small dingy?'

'Will we have to make two trips Bernard?'

'Not atall, sure we'll all fat in na problem,' he replies.

A vision of my bike and all my gear sinking to the bottom of Carlingford Lough on only day two flashes across my eyes, but the two boys know what they are doing and a couple of minutes later we are ashore, and I am pushing my bike up the narrow concrete slipway into Ulster and my home County of Down.

To say that I'm excited would be an understatement when I see the signpost that says: 'Welcome to Greencastle County Down.'

An American diplomat once said that 'Northern Ireland is like Malaria, once it's in your blood stream you never get rid of it'. I can certainly empathise with that as excitedly I push my bike up the slipway and into the province of Ulster.

> *'Ulster the fifth part of Ireland is a large Province, woody, fenny, in some parts fertile, in other parts barren, but in al parts greene and pleasant to behold, and exceedingly stoared with Cattell.*
>
> Fynes Morrison in *'An Itinerary Containing the Ten Yeeres Travell'*

A little bit of Irish history is essential here, before I start my journey into the county of my birth. From the 12th Century, the whole island of Ireland was ruled from London, with a large percentage of the population opposed to British rule. Many bloody conflicts occurred during that period between the Irish people and their English landlords.

The Easter Rising in Dublin on 23 April 1916 finally convinced the English Government to acknowledge that their governance in Ireland had completely broken down. It was to be another four years however, before Liberal Prime Minister Herbert Asquith recommended that Ireland should be freed from British rule.

On 23 December 1920 the Government of Ireland Act became law. The Act partitioned Ireland into two self-governing areas with the six north-eastern counties forming Northern Ireland, whilst the larger part of the country formed Southern Ireland. Both territories were to remain part of the United Kingdom of Great Britain and Ireland.

The Act created two home rule parliaments and divided Ireland on a twenty-six-county basis. Northern Ireland was created with the six counties of Down, Antrim, Armagh, Fermanagh, Londonderry and Tyrone remaining within the United Kingdom.

Prior to 1920, the province of Ulster was made up of nine counties, but the Act effectively chopped off Donegal, Cavan and Monaghan leaving them in the republic, but of course, this has caused endless confusion over the last 100 years. The Ulster rugby team is chosen from the nine counties whilst the Northern Ireland football team is chosen from just the six. Confused? So am I.

Ulster has always been proud of its famous sons and daughters. The list is endless – six Nobel prize-winners, including poet Seamus Heaney from London/Derry, awarded the Nobel Prize for literature in 1995. Seventeen American presidents have Ulster origins. Writers such as C.S. Lewis and Brian Moore were all proud Ulstermen, as was Louis MacNeice.

From the world of entertainment, come actors such as Kenneth Branagh, Liam Neeson, James Nesbitt and Adrian Dunbar, along with Van Morrison, James Galway and Barry Douglas.

The pop group Ash hail from the province, a group who all went to my school in Downpatrick. From the world of sport, Alex Higgins, Lady Mary Peters, Harry Gregg, Eddie Irvine, Barry McGuigan, the late Joey Dunlop, and George Best were all born and educated in Ulster.

From the medical world, Professor Frank Pantridge from County Down invented the portable defibrillator in the Royal Victoria Hospital in 1965. Pantridge had been a Japanese prisoner of war along with my own father during WW2 in the far east. On his return to Belfast, he was convinced that if defibrillators could be put into ambulances, then many more lives could be saved. It took him more than a decade to convince the British authorities, but of course today portable defibrillators are everywhere. Blatant plug here for my biography of Pantridge published by Pen & Sword called *Frank Pantridge MC – Japanese Prisoner of War and Inventor of the Portable Defibrillator.*

Greencastle, (not to be confused with another Greencastle in county Tyrone) is the most southerly village in Ulster. A small, isolated cluster of houses with around 200 inhabitants, lying at the south-eastern extremity of County Down, was a very strategic military fortress guarding the entrance to Carlingford Lough during the 13th.

Thanking Bernard and Pat for their help in getting me across the Lough, I set off out of Greencastle along the Pier Road towards Kilkeel. The sun is shining, and I fairly hum along the narrow road past the disused airfield at Cranfield, an airfield that I remember well from my youth. My dad would take me to motor car racing on Cranfield airfield in the 1950s. The airfield was built in 1942 during the height of WW2 and as with other airfields in Northern Ireland, the site took up a large part of good agricultural land.

Robert Cromie, a native of County Down and a journalist and novelist, wrote about this section of coastline in the Wheel World Magazine in 1882:

> *The southern coast of County Down, if wanting in the wild grandeur of the western seaboard of Ireland, possess a variety of scene quite peculiar to itself, and eminently picturesque. Rarely are such pleasing contracts of landscape met with in such close proximity, and if the portion of the coast referred to falls short in point of heroic outline, there is a wonderful softness, one might say grace, of contour in the Mourne Range which charms and delights the eye; a voluptuous tenderness in the wavy line of Slieve Donard which grows on one and becomes from familiarity even more enjoyable.*

Half an hour of easy cycling and I'm approaching the small fishing port of Kilkeel. With a population of around 6,500, Kilkeel is known as the 'capital of the Kingdom of Mourne.' With its small compact harbour, it has been home to Ireland's largest fishing fleet for several centuries and is the main distribution point for the delicious Mourne potatoes grown in the fertile fields in the foothills of the mountains. Kilkeel harbour was always a lively place back in the 1950s and 60s when the catch of herrings and prawns were landed.

The Greencastle Road comes to an end in the centre of the town and soon I'm on the A2 heading towards Newcastle. The road hugs the cliff tops with superb views across the Irish sea towards the Isle of Man, as it passes through the small villages of Ballymartin, Annalong and Mullartown. The vast expanse of the Mountains of Mourne sweep upwards away to my left in their bleak and majestic splendour, a mountain range made famous by Percy French in 1896 when he composed the song 'Where the Mountains of Mourne Sweep Down to the Sea.'

Oh, Mary, this London's a wonderful sight,
With people all working by day and by night.
Sure, they don't sow potatoes, nor barley, nor wheat,
But there's gangs of them digging for gold in the street.
At least when I asked them that's what I was told,
So I just took a hand at this digging for gold,
But for all that I found there I might as well be
Where the Mountains o' Mourne sweep down to the sea.

The Mournes are the second most famous mountain range in Ireland, after the MacGillycuddy Reeks in County Kerry. The Mournes were a favourite haunt of the celebrated writer C.S. Lewis who described them as:

> *... steep and compact and pointed and jagged. They seem to have nothing to do with the little hills and cottages that divide you from them. And sometimes they look blue, sometimes violet; but quite often they look transparent - as if huge sheets of gauze had been cut into mountainous shapes and hung up there so that you could see through them the light of the invisible sea at their backs.*

The Mournes made such an impression on Lewis that they were the inspiration for his magic Kingdom of Narnia. Lewis loved the dramatic and rugged landscapes of Northern Ireland, from the Mourne's to the romantic ruins of Dunluce Castle in County Antrim, the land inspired him to imagine, dream and wonder.

C. S. Lewis returned to the Mournes as a young man in 1915 for an Easter holiday and wrote a poem:

Cold, snow pure wells
Sweet with the spring tide's scent
Forsaken fells
That I only frequent-
And uplands bare
Would call for me above,
Were I not there
To roam the hills I love
For I alone
Have loved their loneliness:
None else hath known
Nor seen the goodliness
Of the green hills of Down
The soft low hills of Down.

The second highest mountain range Ireland, the Mournes, with their eleven towering, rounded peaks cover an area of about 200 square miles. With names such as Slieve Lamagan, Slieve Commedagh, Slieve Bearnagh and Slieve Donard, they make up a veritable wonderland in an area of exquisite beauty where huge desolate valleys sweep as far as the eye can see. The peaks are all over 600 metres in height with Donard the highest at nearly 850 metres.

By the 1920s, when the city of Belfast's population was expanding rapidly, an additional source of fresh water was needed. The Mourne area, with its abundant rainfall was a logical place for the planners to look towards, and in 1928 an ambitious scheme was drawn up to build a dam in the Silent Valley, a mere three miles away up to my left. Five years later in 1933 Belfast was drawing thirty million gallons a day from the reservoir.

The A2 coast road from Kilkeel towards Newcastle drops away gently making for easy cycling. The mountains rise steeply upwards to my left, whilst to my right the sea glistens and sparkles in the bright late morning sunlight. Steep rocky cliffs fall away down to the shimmering deep purple sea where it rumbles and crashes onto the rocks below. The outline of the Isle of Man, a mere thirty miles across the Irish Sea is clearly visible in the morning sunshine.

Soon I'm cruising down through Annalong, another one of those small Ulster fishing towns that dots this spectacular coastline, with its handful of shops and pubs clustering around its small compact harbour. It was here that as a child I often spent a pleasant afternoon with my family back in the 1960s slurping on a poke. (Let me explain the use of that word: in this part of the world if you want an ice cream, you don't ask for a 'cornet' or a 'wafer', you ask for a 'poke' or a 'slider'. I've never fully understood where these two words for an ice cream originate, but I can only assume that that you 'poked' the ice cream into the cornet and 'slid' the wafer out of a stainless-steel holder called a slider.

We would then have a fish supper fried in traditional Irish fat before setting off for home.

I'm salivating at the thought of one of those fish suppers washed down with a pint of the black stuff, but the day is 'wearing on' as they say in these parts, and I push on towards Newcastle.

Half an hour later and I'm passing over the Bloody Bridge, no not me swearing from the efforts of the last few hours, but the name given to a bridge that carries the A2 over a rocky ravine a couple of miles from Newcastle.

There are many stories about how the bridge got its name. The most commonly accepted one is that in 1641, at the instigation of the Irish chieftain Sir Conn Magennis, a number of Protestant prisoners, taken by the Irish at Newry, were being brought under escort to Newcastle in exchange for Irish prisoners. The Irish commander, hearing that he was to be attacked at Newcastle (or learning that the Irish prisoners held there had been hanged), executed and drove over the rocks at Bloody Bridge as many as 50 of his captives – hence the name 'The Bloody Bridge'.

Despite its rocky and dangerous shoreline, this section of the county Down coast was a haven for smugglers during the 18th and early 19th centuries. It is littered with small, isolated beaches from where goods could be landed and moved quickly up into the shelter of the foothills of the Mournes. The smugglers using small boats landed cargoes such as wines, spirits, tobacco, silks, spices, tea coffee, sugar, leather and soap. They carried their haul up through the mountains on the backs of small ponies up using a track known as the Brandy Pad, a route that climbs steeply up from the sea near the Bridge into the mountains.

Leaving the Bridge to the smugglers, I pedal on down towards Newcastle, a seaside town that nestles in a stunningly beautiful location at the very foot of Slieve Donard.

Stopping briefly at the open-air swimming pool that overlooks the harbour, my thoughts wander back to the late 1950s when I learnt to swim in this very pool. Even in mid-summer the water was icy cold, but such was my determination to master the strokes, that I ignored the cold and ploughed up and down. My parents keep an eye on me from deck chairs on the pool side, suitably wrapped up in big coats and scarves - no lifeguards in those days.

Putting nostalgia to one side, I remount and set off again towards the town centre. Suddenly I feel myself starting to rise and fall with each turn of the pedals. Stopping by the roadside, I look down at my back wheel and am horrified to discover that it is no longer the perfectly spherical object it was at the start of the day but is now somewhat oval shaped.

Changing from my cleated cycling shoes into my training shoes I push my bike towards Newcastle town centre. As it turns out, I'm very fortunate in that this disaster occurs only a mile or so from a good-sized town, if it had happened miles out in the country I would have been in 'sh1t' as they say. Pushing my bike along the pavement I stop a lady and ask, 'excuse me madam, is there a bicycle shop in Newcastle?'

Ah sur, there is one at the far end of town, just near the bus station.' she replies to my great relief. Thanking her I continue pushing my loaded steed up through the busy main street.

Wiki Wiki Wheels is situated at the end of Donard Street, and I'm surprised to see rows of lawn mowers lined up outside. Perhaps the lady got confused between bikes and lawn mowers? If my bike is irreparable, perhaps I can finish the trip on a lawn mower?

'I'm cycling round Ireland and I've got a bit of a problem with my back wheel it seems to have buckled,' I say to the man behind the counter.

'We should be able to help you sir, let's tak a wee look,' he replies. 'Ye need a new back wheel, that un's not up to the job of carrying your own body weight on the back, ye need a top quality whan to tak the weight. I can fit one for you, but t'll cost ye aboot £95 including a new chain and back sprocket set and it'll tak aboot an hour or so.'

With little choice, I leave my bike in the tender loving care of Tom in Wiki Wiki Wheels and stroll up past the bus station towards the seafront, where I spend a very pleasant hour sitting on a bench slurping an ice cream whilst watching the sea wash in over the wide expanse of Newcastle Bay. At least I'm getting a good hour's rest after a hard morning's cycling.

Over to my left the Slieve Donard Hotel glistens in the early afternoon sun. The Donard was built in the late nineteenth century by the Belfast and County Down Railway Company to provide its clients with a luxurious hotel at the end of its line from Belfast. At that time, it cost around £3 for a week's full board including train travel. Charlie Chaplin stayed here in 1921 after divorcing his wife and indeed the hotel still has a Chaplin's Bar.

During the late 1970s when the troubles were at their peak, the Donard was bombed four times resulting in it being nicknamed the 'Titanic.'

The Donard is situated in a wonderful location with the Irish Sea washing up to its grand entrance on one side, whilst the undulating sand dunes of the world-famous Royal County Down golf course dominate the other – all overlooked by a huge, towering mountain.

With a gleaming new wheel in place and £95 out of my budget, I clip my panniers back on and head on east out of Newcastle along the A2 towards Dundrum. Twenty minutes later, and I'm cycling along Dundrum's single main street.

Sitting on a small hillock overlooking the town up to my left, Dundrum Castle is an impressive structure. The castle was built around the beginning of the thirteenth century by John de Courcy when he ruled the province and dominated most of Ulster.

A mile or so out of Dundrum and the road begins to incline steeply up Mount Panther Hill. Slipping down through the gears, I struggle to turn over the pedals and it's a relief when I eventually reach the summit and collapse in a heap on the grass verge. Wiping the sweat from my brow and glugging from my water bottle I glance around me. Away to my left above some tall trees, I can just make out the roof of Mount Panther House, a huge Georgian mansion built in the 1700s and owned for many years by one of the area's most well-known families, the Annesleys.

By now it's late afternoon and with at least an hour's cycling left to reach the farm McCann, I drag my weary body back into the saddle and set off again towards Clough. From the top of Mount Panther hill, the road drops sharply downhill and its bliss to freewheel downhill after the previous climb. The bliss does not last long before once again I have to click down through the gears and force my aching legs up the steep hill into the village of Clough. Its name originated from the stone castle that stands on top of a mound that was used as a Norman motte.

At the village I turn right onto the Blackstaff Road and carry on along the A2 towards the villages of Tyrella and Minerstown. The sunshine of earlier in the day has now turned into threatening black skies, and as I approach Ballykinler it begins to rain heavily. Donning my waterproofs for the first time on the trip, I put my head down over the handlebars and press on with the rain trickling down the back of my neck and dripping off my nose.

Passing the sign for Tyrella beach, my thoughts drift back to sunny summer days back in the 1950s when I would swim in the sea and collect shells along the golden sands. Tyrella beach is one of the safest and cleanest in Ireland

and has had Blue Flag status for many years. Just off this section of beach in 1846, the Ocean Liner SS Great Britain ran aground on its way from Liverpool to New York. Fortunately, all the 180 passengers and 85 crew were rescued without loss of life.

With my overnight stop now only about an hour or so away, I push on through Minerstown where, through the mist, I catch a glimpse of the black and yellow finger of St John's Point Lighthouse. A well-known landmark on this part of the county Down coast it has been warning mariners of the dangers of a shallow rocky promontory jutting out into the Irish Sea for many years. Stopping for a few minutes at Rossglass, I look through the mist, back over the vast expanse of Dundrum Bay towards the Mournes from when I have just come. The view on a good day is stunning as I well remember from my childhood days, but today it's a matter of using my imagination. I get quite emotional, as this area is where my mother's family are from, she was born in 1913 just a few miles away from where I'm standing.

Wiping the tears away, I turn inland off the A2 at Rossglass onto the Ballylig road. I've now got only a few miles left to pedal until I reach the farm of good friends Derek and Frances McCann in Ballee.

As usual I'm welcomed with open arms at the farm McCann – one hundred acres of lush, green countryside among the rolling drumlins of County Down, a virtual oasis of peace and tranquillity. The farm has been in the McCann family for several centuries and has produced some of the finest mutton and beef in Ireland.

After another one Frances's wonderful dinners, lots of cups of strong tea and a great deal of reminiscing, I sink into a deep sleep after the rigours of day two.

Day's statistics: 62.5 miles – Average speed – 12mph – Time taken – 5hours 10 minutes – Max speed – 29.9mph

Note: Almost two years after I made my trip, I read that on 31st January 2002 a mussel fishing vessel sank in Carlingford Lough causing the death of crewman. I was concerned that it might have been Bernard and Pat's vessel, but it turned out to be another mussel fishing boat, much to my relief.

Chapter 6

Day 3 – Ballee to Belfast (42 miles)

It's a bright sunny morning when I throw back the curtains on day three of my trip and head downstairs for one of Frances's Ulster fry breakfasts. Quite frankly they are to die for, bacon, sausage, egg, mushrooms, tomatoes, black and white puddings, fried bread and soda farls (the word farl is a shorter form of fardel, the word once used in some parts of Lowland Scotland for a three-cornered cake), all washed down with huge cups of strong tea – bliss.

The Ulster fry is of course famous the world over and cannot be beaten when it was cooked to perfection by my mother back in the early 1950s and 60s. The Ulster fry is well summed up by Florence Mary McDowell when she traced the history of the dish in her book Other Days Around Me:

> *The Ulster Fry has a long and solid history. Its popularity was probably due to two things – firstly, the housewife usually had only an open fire, so more sophisticated methods of cooking were not hers to command; and gory work, there would be bacon and hams to be salted or hung up inside the chimney to smoke. The pork ribs, liver and offal would make tasty eating in the meantime for the family and neighbours, and there would be plenty of lard for the Ulster Fry. Little of the pig was wasted, even the feet being boiled for succulent eating. Pigs' trotters are possibly not everyone's fancy, but they had their following 'secondly, every man, woman or child who could do so tried to rear a pig on scraps and chat potatoes and whatever the free-rooting pig could find on its own hoking expeditions. Often it was a crowl, the runt of a litter, given away by a farmer to anyone who wanted to take the trouble to rear it. After the local pig killer had done his.*

After a sumptuous McCann breakfast, it's time for my photo call. The local *Down Recorder* had got wind of my trip and their photographer calls to take my picture with Derek. Picture taken, I bid the McCanns farewell and head on for Belfast, Northern Ireland's capital city. Fifteen minutes later and I'm cycling into Downpatrick.

You will have to excuse me dear reader as I shamelessly expand on my emotional cycle through the town where I was born and went to school.

Named after Saint Patrick, Downpatrick is a busy market town nestling snugly in a hollow between two hills or drumlins (derived from the Irish word droimnín, an elongated hill in the shape of an inverted spoon or half-buried egg formed by glacial ice), with the River Quoile running close by on its route towards the Irish Sea. Down Cathedral dominates the town from a wooded hill at the top of English Street where a huge granite slab brought down from the Mournes marks the spot where, tradition has it, Saint Patrick is buried. Laid to ruins in 1538, the cathedral was restored at the end of the eighteenth century by Charles Lilly.

Cycling down into the town centre, I stop briefly at a barber's shop. Now I'm sure you are wondering why I want to get a haircut so early in the trip, but the significance is that it was the barbers where, during the 1950s and early 1960s, Tommy Miley pulled my hair out whilst telling me his life story. Going for my monthly haircut to Tommy was almost as bad as going to the dentist. Any of you who remember the old hand operated clippers they used at that time will understand. If I recall correctly, it was one shilling for the dubious pleasure of Tommy Miley's company. Gazing up at the pole brought at wry smile to my face when a certain memory popped into my head. I must have been about 11 when my mother gave me a shilling to get my hair cut at Tommy's after school. On the way home I had completely forgotten about the haircut and when I found the shilling in my pocket, I promptly spent it on wagon wheels. My mum wasn't best pleased.

Four medieval streets fan out from the centre of Downpatrick – Scotch Street, Irish Street, English Street and Church Street. I've always wondered why there is no Welsh street. English Street leads up to the Southwell School, the second oldest school in Ireland, founded in 1685 by Hugo Southwell a prominent citizen of the town, a school that I attended for one year when I was five years old, just before it closed, and where I wet my pants on my first day.

A few minutes later I stop again at the church I attended 'religiously' during my formative years to pay homage to the memorial stone of my mother and father. The stone is located at the east end of the church overlooking the British Legion club where my father spent many happy hours. After shedding a tear, I remount and cycle on down Church Street towards the war memorial before swinging right onto Strangford Road and on towards the Quoile Quay.

As it's my hometown, I'm making more stops this morning than I normally would, and I slam on the brakes by the old quayside. Up until the 1940s sailing ships and steamers docked at the Quoile Quay, bringing timber, coal and slate to the town, but today it is a quiet tranquil spot where families spend Sunday afternoons picnicking on the grassy banks of the river. Pleasant memories of sailing on the Quoile come flooding back as I sit for a few minutes on the grassy bank by the now disused and crumbling slipway.

Remounting, I press on along the very familiar A25 towards Strangford. Up at the top of a drumlin to my right, I catch my first glimpse of Saint Patrick, not a reincarnation of the saint, but a 10-metre-high statue that gazes down over Strangford Lough. It's well worth the twenty-minute walk up to the top of Slieve Patrick for the stupendous views across a wide swathe of County Down, Strangford Lough and the Ards peninsula to the north, the Lecale peninsula and the Irish sea to the east and the Mourne Mountains to the south. This statue of Patrick was erected on the site in 1932 to commemorate the 1500th anniversary of his landing on a nearby shore in AD432, where at the nearby Saul Church, he is reported to preached for the first time in Ireland.

After another six miles of easy cycling along the A25 I pass the entrance to Castleward, the home of the Ward family since 1570. The 850-acre walled demesne was given to the National Trust in 1952. The estate is of personal interest to me as it is said that 1852, twenty-five families living and working on the estate were evicted from their homes because allegedly their settlement was ruining the view of the then 'lord and lady' of the manor. The families, including two Lowrys were put on a boat to America never to be seen or heard of again. Of course, this story is anecdotal only and some experts believe that the story is made up.

No time for any more sightseeing though and I press on into the charming little village of Strangford. Nestling neatly in a small bay on the west side of a narrow tidal race, (Strang Fjord the violent inlet from old Norse) was given its name due to the three hundred and fifty million tons of water that pours into the lough at a rate of ten knots and back out again every tidal change.

Of Strangford Lough, Rynne wrote back in 1955:

> *Strangford Lough is just a bottle of agitated water, a service to none and fun only to hardy sportsmen and a few doughty owners of pleasure-ships.*

Tradition has it that in 432AD when St Patrick was making his way back to Ireland, he had intended to sail up the coast to county Antrim where, as a young slave, he had tended flocks for six years on Slemish mountain, but his small boat was pushed into Strangford Lough by the strong tide.

A small car ferry crosses this 'agitated' stretch of water thirty-two times a day from Strangford to Portaferry and back, a service that has been operating for over four centuries. Prior to the launch of the current car ferry in 1969, it was a small passenger ferry for foot passengers only.

When I arrive at the quayside the vessel has not yet left Portaferry, and as I have at least 15 minutes to relax and take in the surroundings, I purchase a 'poke' from a little shop overlooking the harbour called 'Kevin Og.'

Relaxing in the midday sunshine whilst contentedly licking my poke, I gaze out across the turbulent blue waters as the ferry makes its ten-minute journey across the narrows. It seems to move as fast sideways as it does forward as it is swept down the tidal race towards Strangford.

I'm first off the vessel when it docks fifteen minutes later at Portaferry. A small town with a long history, Portaferry dates to the twelfth century when a group of fishermen's cottages were built beside an Anglo-Norman castle overlooking the strategic entrance to Strangford Lough. The opening of Strangford car ferry in 1969, as I mentioned earlier, resulted in a boom for the town. It soon became a bustling place, particularly in the summer months, when Belfast people would make the day trip along the Ards peninsula, have lunch in the quaint little cafés and then take the ferry to Strangford before driving back home along the west side of the lough – a great day out as they say in these parts.

Leaving Portaferry I set off northwards along the A20 on the east side of the lough. Strangford Lough, the largest inlet in the British Isles covering 58 square miles, was designated as Northern Ireland's first Marine Conservation Zone under the introduction of the Marine Act in 2013. Often referred to as Ulster's Killarney, this superb stretch of water eighteen miles long has a shoreline of eighty miles and is often referred to as Ulster's Killarney. It is dotted with 366 islands, one for every day of the year plus an extra one for Easter Sunday it is said. The Ards peninsula, along which I'm now cycling, is a finger of land some four miles wide that divides the lough from the Irish Sea. Robert Lloyd Praeger summed up its beauty when he toured Ireland 1937:

> *The fifteen-mile strip that lies between Strangford Lough and the Irish sea, known as the Ards, shows Down at its best – all tiled fields and white cottages and little winding roads, and a low flowery coastline with alternating points of sharp upturned slates and bays of fine grey sand.*

The Ards peninsula is littered with small villages and hamlets and with the wind on my back I fairly scoot along and soon arrive at the pretty little village of Kircubbin. Fifteen minutes later and I'm entering Greyabbey, where a Cistercian monastery was built nearby in 1193 by Affreca, the wife of that man again, John de Courcy. Set in parkland, the monastery, a mass of sandstone ruins surrounded by huge trees, must have been an impressive building back in the twelfth century.

Soon I'm cycling past the entrance to Mount Stewart Estate, the eighteenth-century home of Lord Castlereagh, one of Britain's most influential foreign ministers during the Napoleonic wars. Mount Stewart is now under the auspices of the National Trust with many thousands of people visiting the superb house and gardens each year.

A few miles further on I stop for a drink at the Newtownards Sailing Club, where in 1964, I won the Northern Ireland Junior GP 14 sailing Championships. Nostalgia again kicks in as I gaze out across the sparkling waters of the lough.

Two miles later and I'm approaching the town of Newtownards, or Ards as the locals call it. With a population of around 24,000 Ards is a busy modern shopping town about a mile or so inland from the northern end of the lough. The imposing Scrabo Tower at 135ft high, a nineteenth century lookout tower standing on Scrabo Hill, provides wide views over the town and is a landmark that can be seen from afar. By now it is approaching the late afternoon rush hour, and the A20 out of Ards is particularly busy. Traffic whizzes past me at a great speed as I drop through the gears, put my head down over the handlebars and pedal up the steep slope towards Dundonald. Passing a lay-by, I'm astonished when I hear a loud voice, 'de ye wan a beg?' Lifting my head, a young lad sitting on the tailgate of a lorry loaded with potatoes and garden ornaments (a curious mix) smiles and waves at me, the humour of the Ulster wit never ceases to amaze. With a quick 'no thanks mate,' I grit my teeth and push on up the steep slope.

It's a massive relief to reach the summit and as the road levels out, I get my first views of the city of Belfast and the suburb of Dundonald. I'm sure the 'Dundonaldions' (my word I think) will rise in anger when I say it is now part of Belfast, but as is the case with many cities in the British Isles, town boundaries have become somewhat blurred over the years.

The volume of traffic on the Upper Newtownards Road begins to increase as I approach the Ulster Hospital, which has seen more than its fair share of casualties during the Troubles. I have to keep my wits about me as lorries and cars whizz past at a rate of knots, but at least I can draw comfort in the fact that I have not far to go to the Ulster Hospital A&E if I come a cropper.

Taking another well-earned rest at the entrance to Stormont Castle, I prop my bike against the statue of Sir Edward Henry Carson. Stormont Castle is the home of Northern Ireland's parliament and is a building that has probably had more exposure on national television than any other public building in the UK. Carson was a barrister, judge and leader of the Irish Unionist Alliance and Ulster Unionist party between 1910 and 1921 when he held numerous positions in the UK Cabinet. In 1915 he entered the war cabinet of Herbert Asquith as Attorney-General. Carson was defeated in his ambition to maintain Ireland as a whole in union with Great Britain, but his leadership, however, was celebrated by some for securing a continued place in the United Kingdom for the six north-eastern counties, albeit under a devolved Parliament of Northern Ireland that neither he nor his fellow unionists had sought.

Waving Carson goodbye, I turn left onto the A55 Belfast ring road and head for my pre-booked accommodation in the Ravenhill Guest House at the junction of the Ormeau and Ravenhill roads. I'm welcomed by Roger Nicholson and when I hear his North-East of England accent I enquire where is from: 'I'm originally from Sunderland, have you been there?' he replies.

Of course, I'm delighted, as I spent three years in at College in Sunderland and I know the town (now a city) well. Like myself, Roger is a big Sunderland AFC supporter. We get on like a house on fire.

Day's statistics: 42.4 miles – Average speed – 12.2mph – Time taken – 3hours 45 minutes – Max speed – 32.7mph

Chapter 7

Day 4 – Belfast to Carnlough (56 miles)

Day four dawns bright and warm and after an excellent breakfast at the Ravenhill I bid Roger and his wife farewell, load up the bike and set off down the Ravenhill Road towards Belfast city centre. At the end of the Ravenhill Road, rather than crossing the East Bridge over the Lagan, I decide to take a small detour along the Albertbridge Road to the Newtownards Road.

The Newtownards Road is a very staunch loyalist area, demonstrated by the vivid murals with political and religious undertones painted on gable ends of houses and shops. Cycling down towards the city centre, I nearly come a cropper several times whilst gazing up at these truly incredible works of art.

Crossing the Queens Bridge that straddles the River Lagan, I enter the fifth county of my trip, Antrim. I pause for a breather near the Albert Memorial clock, a memorial to Queen Victoria's late Prince Consort, Prince Albert.

The clock is Ulster's leaning Tower of Pisa, some four and a half feet off base, apparently due to being built on swampland or 'sleech' in the 1860s.

The advantage of being on a bicycle in Belfast is that I'm able to gaze up at the fantastic prime Victorian architecture that might pass you by if you drive through this busy city. On the corner of Donegal Square and Donegal Place stands the Robinson and Cleaver department store, one of the most upmarket shops in Belfast when we used to visit the city in the 1960s.

Northern Ireland's capital city lies on one of the most natural and beautiful locations in the British Isles. The River Lagan splits it in half as it meanders through the centre into Belfast Lough and the Irish Sea beyond.

To the north of the city the high basalt ridges of the 1,000-foot Cave Hill rise steeply and menacingly, casting a shadow over its citizens. Many people who have not visited Belfast will almost certainly have preconceived ideas about the city as a dull, dour place inhabited by two divided communities of dull dour people whose only purpose in life is to obliterate each other, but in modern day Belfast that is far from the case.

In 1855 Rynne made this perception when he wrote of Belfast:

'It has no aristocracy, no culture, no leisure.
The greater part of the city is as drab as Glasgow.'

This may well have been the case as Rynne describes it in 1855, but 160 years later, Belfast has changed and is now one of the most vibrant cities in the United Kingdom. Whilst many deprived areas still exist, others have been improved to a high standard, especially the Laganside area that has been redeveloped, with high quality apartment and office blocks sprouting up all along the river.

Belfast was the birthplace of the respected writer C.S. Lewis, and he gives us a different perspective to Rynne on the city. Growing up in a city rich in maritime and industrial history was one of his proudest childhood memories, with the sights and sounds embedding themselves in his imagination. Lewis loved what was known as the 'Belfast Symphony' – the continual throb and stammer of the great shipyards.

During the Second World War Belfast suffered badly from Nazi bombing. The Harland and Wolfe shipyards and the Shorts aircraft factories were prime targets and during the first week of May 1941, a huge force of German bombers attacked the docks. For two days Belfast took an almighty battering with more than 1,000 people losing their lives. I remember my mother telling me about the terror she felt as the bombs dropped when she was working as a housemaid for a Belfast clergyman in a large house on the Malone Road. She told me that they would hide in the cellars as the bombs rained down on the city.

I can't leave Belfast without a vote of thanks to the man who invented the pneumatic tyres that are humming beneath me. A mere half a mile away in May Street, a man called John Boyd Dunlop was said to have invented the first pneumatic tyres in 1888. Dunlop was a vet who had a nine-year-old son, and the boy was constantly complaining about the uncomfortable ride on the solid tyres of his tricycle as he cycled along the cobbled streets of Belfast. He removed the solid rubber tyres and attached air filled canvas tubes to the rims. Whilst Dunlop has always been credited with the invention, it had actually been invented forty-four years earlier in Scotland by a Robert Thomson who had already patented a design for a pneumatic tyre on horse drawn carriages.

Enough of the history and back to the cycling. I remount, leave the city behind and cycle on along the Shore Road towards Carrickfergus. The Shore Road hugs the north bank of Belfast Lough and is quiet this morning. This road used to be very busy before the adjacent four lane M22 was opened in 1973, as it carried most of the vehicles heading north towards Larne and London/Derry.

Glancing across the Lagan, I catch my first glimpse of Sampson and Goliath, the two huge sleeping metal giant cranes that cast their shadows across the river. The cranes are testament to the great era of shipbuilding during the late 19th and early 20th centuries when Harland and Wolf led the world. These iconic structures have been featured in many documentaries and films set in Ulster in recent years and named after the Biblical figures Samson and Goliath.

Harland and Wolfe was the shipyard that built the Titanic, a ship that took three years to build and that survived for only thirteen days after leaving these docks. When the Titanic struck an iceberg and sank on her maiden voyage across the Atlantic in 1912 1,500 people lost their lives and Belfast went into mourning. More than 15,000 local people had been involved in the building of the ship and many, along with its designer Thomas Andrews, tragically lost their lives.

(It wasn't until Titanic Belfast, a visitor attraction, opened in 2012 that Belfast cashed in on the Titanic story when the Titanic Centre was built on the site of its construction. The building contains more than 12,000 square metres of floor space, most of which is occupied by a series of galleries, private function rooms and community facilities.)

The sun is shining and with a strong following wind, I fairly speed along towards Carrickfergus. The Lough's foam-topped waves glisten in the morning sun as they scurry away towards the Irish Sea and Scotland beyond. Rising up to my left the Cave Hill, known in these parts as Napoleon's Nose, because of its likeness to the profile of the French emperor, looms over Belfast. It is said that the Cave Hill gave Jonathan Swift the inspiration for Gulliver in his book Gulliver's Travels as it resembled the head of a sleeping giant.

Belfast Lough is alive with yachts and boats as I cycle through the villages of Whiteabbey, Jordanstown and Greenisland. Brightly coloured sails tack from one side to the other, and once again nostalgia kicks in as my thoughts drift back to my teenage years in the early 1960s, when I raced my Enterprise dinghy out of the Holywood and Royal North of Ireland Yacht clubs just across the Lough.

Feeling rather envious of the sailors out on the water, I put my head down over the handlebars, slip up through the gears and concentrate on the task in hand.

A few minutes later, I'm forced to slam on the brakes just in time to avoid crashing into a milk float that pulls out of a side street directly into my path.

'Oh, sorry by, didn't see ye. Sure: it's a grand day by isn't it,' says the driver cheerfully as if nothing has happened. 'De you wanna pinta milk?'

For those of you have not been to the North of Ireland, the word 'by' is a very common expression, often thrown into sentences and indeed often used more than once in a sentence. It means 'boy' the other person to whom you are talking. Whilst we are on Ulster expressions, another common one often heard is 'whad about ye?' Which means in effect 'how are you today?' and often tagged on to the end is 'auld han' which means 'how are you today, experienced person or friend'. Don't ask me to expand further as to the origins of such colloquialisms.

Declining the driver's offer of a pint of milk, I press on. The town of Carrickfergus, eleven miles from the centre of Belfast, is situated at the north-eastern end of Belfast Lough just as the lough enters the Irish sea and before the coastline sweeps northwards. It's Northern Ireland's oldest town and indeed one of the oldest towns in Ireland. Carrick as it is abbreviated to, was the main port for the north-east coast of Ireland for many years, long before Belfast took over that mantle. In 1912 the people of Carrick turned out in their thousands to watch as the Titanic made its first ever journey up the Lough from its construction dock just a few miles upriver. The ill-fated passenger liner was anchored overnight just off the coast of Carrickfergus before continuing on its journey of doom.

The town is dominated by an impressive Castle, one of the largest and most well-preserved castles in Ireland. Built in 1178 by that man again, John de Courcy, with just a little financial help from King Henry II, it was one of the most important castles in Ireland during the twelfth century due to its command of the entrance to Belfast Lough.

Just a few yards away from the castle stands the statue of William of Orange or King Billy as he affectionately known by Ulster Loyalists. The statue was erected in 1990 to commemorate the fact that he landed at Carrickfergus harbour on 14 June 1690 on his way to fight King James at the Battle of the Boyne. (A battle I mentioned in chapter four.)

After a stop in the castle grounds to grab a sandwich, I head on up the A2 towards Larne. Down to my right is the small village of Boneybefore, a village where the parents of the 7th US president Andrew Jackson lived before emigrating to the Carolinas in 1767. A statue to him stands at the visitor centre in the village.

Cycling past the delightful little village of Eden a street sign catches my eye, 'The Garden of Eden' it proclaims, causing me a little chuckle to myself, the biblical Garden of Eden it ain't. Over to my right, Kilroot Power Station with its two huge chimneys rising like fingers pointing to the heavens casts an ugly shadow over the village, its two olive green buildings clinging to the base of the chimneys like wartime bunkers.

Another one of Ulster's famous sons, the novelist Jonathan Swift, was the Anglican prebend in Kilroot from 1694 to 1696 and it was here that he supposedly conceived A Tale of a Tub whilst skimming stones across the Irish sea. It is also said that the views across the Lough from Kilroot to the Copeland Islands gave him the idea for the island of Laputa in Gullivers Travels.

Swinging northwards up the coast road, the wind has now changed direction and turned into a northerly gale. It's now a huge effort to even turn over the pedals in my lowest gear.

For a mile or so I get some respite from the wind behind a battered old van loaded high with household possessions, two televisions, a bed, a sofa, a battered old mattress and collection of black plastic bags are stacked precariously on the back. Whilst it is a welcome relief from the wind, I'm reluctant to get too close to this 'do it yourself' removals van as I visualise my trip ending here and now under a pile of old furniture. The 'luxury' of this unexpected shelter soon ends when the van turns off the main road, and I am once again left to the mercy of the howling gale.

For the next hour, I grind out the miles up the A2 passing through the lovely seaside town of Whitehead and on along the west shore of Larne Lough. At the hamlet of Magheramorne, a large sign catches my eye. 'Oxygen Therapy Centre' it reads. Gasping for breath and needing some oxygen I swing off the road and into the car park. Chaining my bike against a small sapling I clunk into the reception. There, I am greeted by a lovely lady who informs me that the Oxygen Therapy Centre is run by East Antrim Therapy, a charity that provides regular pressurised oxygen treatment for a variety of ailments, particularly for MS sufferers.

'It has been discovered that by increasing the oxygen supply to MS sufferers at high pressure, it eases their symptoms. The principle is like the treatment given to divers who encounter the "bends" when they come to the surface quickly after being at great depths. Patients are sealed inside what looks like a diving bell and pressured to the equivalent of depths of up to 200 feet where they then breathe pure oxygen for an hour or so', she informs me.

After a most welcome twenty-minute rest and making a donation to this worthwhile charity, I saddle up again and press on towards Larne. To my right across Larne Lough at the very tip of the Islandmagee peninsula, I can just make out the ugly fingers of another of those dreaded power stations, Ballylumford, a station that provides half of Northern Ireland's electricity. The sight of this monstrosity is the first uninspiring view that visitors to Ulster get when they enter Larne Lough on a cross-channel ferry.

Gliding down the hill into Larne I can just make out the huge ferries in the harbour disgorging cars and lorries bound for all parts of Ireland. Larne has been Ulster's main ferry terminal for many years with ferries arriving from Cairnryan and Troon in Scotland on a regular basis. The sea crossing of forty miles is the shortest ferry route from mainland Britain. Today, Larne is renowned as one of Ireland's premier Ports handling over 300,000 freight units a year, as well as 220,000 tourist vehicles and 845,000 passengers. It is operative 24 hours per day, seven days a week, with up to twenty arrivals and departures daily.

The town of Larne has produced many famous sons and daughters over the centuries, including the parents of the novelist Mark Twain before they emigrated across the Atlantic to Missouri. Dave 'boy' McAuley, one of Ireland's former world boxing champions hails from the area. Larne claims to be the birthplace former American president Andrew Johnson. Johnson was conceived in Larne and born in the middle of the Atlantic on an emigrant ship taking his parents to America in 1767. Over 20,000 Ulster-Scots left Larne in that year bound for North America leaving behind what was a very turbulent Ireland.

Leaving the shelter of Larne, I grind out the miles up the A2 into the strong headwind that has been with me since Carrickfergus. The Irish Sea immediately to my right looks like a cavalry battalion of white horses, with the wind whipping the tops off the waves like a giant trying to cool his hot cup of tea.

The Antrim coast was one of William Makepeace Thackeray's favourite parts of Ireland, and he often waxed lyrical about this part of Ulster:

> *If the road from Larne to Glenarm is beautiful, the coast route from the latter place to Cushendall is still more so; and, except peerless Westport, I have seen nothing in Ireland so picturesque as this noble line of coast-scenery. The Antrim coast road… besides being one of the most noble and gallant works of art that is to be seen in any country, is likewise a route highly picturesque and romantic… The road, which almost always skirts the hillside, has been torn sheer through the rock here and there; and immense works of levelling, shovelling, picking, blasting, filling, is going on along the whole line.*

Thackery was not wrong, as the coastline from Larne to Ballycastle is probably one of the most beautiful and rugged coastlines in the whole of Ireland, but its beauty is lost on me at the end of hard day in the saddle as I toil to turn over the pedals.

The road hugs the shoreline as huge, towering cliffs rise away to the left, with triangular signs warning of falling boulders. I get a vision of me and my bike ending up in the sea as I am swept to an icy grave by huge lumps of granite.

Prior to the construction of the Antrim coast road in the 1830s, inhabitants of the area found it easier to sail across the thirty miles to Scotland to trade rather than with their fellow Irish inland over the Glens or down in Belfast.

Struggling on past the Carnfunnock Country Park and through the village of Ballygally into Glenarm, my legs are turning to jelly. Even pedalling in the lowest gear is now a mighty effort, and there is just no way that I will reach my target for the day, Cushendun, some fifteen miles further on.

Stopping for a breather and quick look at my map, the small village of Carnlough 6 miles up ahead, looks like a good option for my overnight stop. Into this howling gale, it takes me another hour to cycle these last six miles and when the 'Welcome to Carnlough' sign appears on the roadside, I breathe a huge sigh of relief.

Up until the early 1960s, Carnlough was a busy little village, mainly due to its harbour where limestone from the quarries in the hills above the town was loaded onto ships for export to Scotland. Today it is a sleepy little place with just a few fishing boats and pleasure craft using the harbour.

With a population of around 2,000, Carnlough's main street is a mere 200 yards long. The only accommodation seems to be the Londonderry Arms, a coaching Inn built in 1848 and it certainly looks out of my price league, so I cycle back along the main street. The only B&B I spot is the Bethany Christian Guest House with a 'vacancies' sign hanging outside.

'Would you like a cup of tea? you look as though you need one,' says the landlady Mrs Aiken, confirming that she has a room available when I ring the bell. Gratefully accepting and not even asking her charges, I wheel my bike into a barn at the rear of the house and collapse exhausted into a comfy chair in the lounge.

After a shower and a quick nap, I recover well enough to venture out for a couple of pints of Guinness and some food. Carnlough is not enamoured with pubs and restaurant and there is very few to choose from, and with the Londonderry Arms menu looking a bit out of my budget, a fish and chip shop a few doors down look's promising for later. Glancing down a side street a sign catches my eye - Waterfall Bar Bushmills Pub of the Year, it proclaims – just what I'm looking for.

It's still early evening, and the Waterfall Bar is quiet when I walk in. Waiting the full two minutes sixteen seconds it takes to pour my pint of Guinness, I try to decipher the conversation between a couple of the locals chatting at the bar. The County Antrim accent is one of the most difficult of all the Irish accents to understand, and even with my roots being not too far away in neighbouring County Down I'm having a problem understanding what they are saying. Not that I'm eavesdropping of course, but it is so quiet that you can hear the conversation.

'Cher boy' keeps cropping up at regular intervals which very roughly translated means 'I'm telling you my friend'. 'Ace won' is also an expression used and it is only later that it dawns on me they are not talking about poker but about the east wind blowing in from the sea.

Taking a seat in the corner of the bar, I open my book and take the first sip of my Guinness when the door opens and a young lady enters, obviously well-known, as she is greeted cheerily by the three men at the bar. A few minutes later she comes over to my table with a pint of Guinness in her hand.

'Mine af I join yu', she says cheerily.

'Not at all,' I reply, gesturing to the three empty chairs.

'May name's Sarah, what's yours? She cheerfully asks.

'I can tell by your accent that you have been away from Northern Ireland for a while, are you on holiday?'

'I'm Cecil and I live in England now but I'm originally from County Down. I'm on a round Ireland cycle ride' I reply.

'By that's some challenge Cecil, gud luck ta you now, ya deserve another pint of Guinness.'

With my fish and chip supper now looming I decline, but Sarah is such good company and very insistent that I succumb to her charms and my second pint of Guinness appears as if by magic.

'Ah sur I'm expectin a cawple of gurl frends shortly, you can wait and meet them. Ye can always get your fish and chips later, they don't close too errly rune here. The girls would love to hear about your trip,' she says.

The atmosphere in the Waterfall is very convivial by now as the locals start to arrive for the evening drinking session.

Half an hour later, Karen and Mary join us, expanding the round to four and the Guinness is now going down faster than the Titanic. Karen is a local community worker in Carnlough, and Mary is a herbalist who works in a shop in Ballymena, about 15 miles inland.

The next couple of hours just fly past as the four of us we solve every problem in the world. The 'craic' is excellent, and the Guinness is flowing freely until I look at my watch – to my horror it is 11.15pm.

'Oh my God girls I haven't eaten since lunchtime and I was going to get a fish supper,' I slur.

'Too late,' they all laugh. 'The chip shop closed 15 minutes ago. You'll 'ave to make do with crisps and nuts, have another pint, sure there's planty af nutrients in the Guinness.'

Slumping back in my chair with a huge grin on my face, I just ignore the fact that I have 60 miles to cycle tomorrow.

Staggering out of the pub at around midnight, Mary says to me, 'Just wait there a minute, Cecil' and dashes off down the street. A few minutes later she returns clutching what I can only describe as a jar of green slime.

'This is great for aching muscles I make it up myself and lots of people say it's brilliant,' she says as she pushes it into my unsteady hands.

Bidding my new-found friends, a slurred goodnight, I make my way rather unsteadily back towards the Bethany Guest House.

The house is very quiet when I approach the front door, and after fumbling with the key and tripping over the step, I crash into the hallway. For some reason I put my finger to my lips and somewhat unsteadily I creep upstairs to my room where I crash out in a Guinness induced deep sleep.

Day's statistics: 55.2 miles – Average speed – 11.2mph – Time taken – 4hours 57 minutes – Max speed – 20.5mph

Chapter 8

Day 5 – Carnlough to Portstewart (55 miles)

My evening in Carnlough's Waterfall Bar was the most enjoyable of the trip so far, but five pints of Guinness on an empty stomach was of course not the ideal preparation for an assault on the hills up to Ballycastle today.

It's now the morning of day five and I feel decidedly rough after the alcoholic excesses of last night. Mrs Aiken's superb Ulster Fry looks and smells wonderful, but my stomach is feeling just a tad fragile after last night's 'session', but with a day's cycling ahead of me I need the calories, so I make the effort to force it down, nonetheless.

Suitably refreshed and fuelled, I load up my gear, settle my bill and am soon on the road heading northwards again. My head is still a bit fuzzy from the 'drink' and I have to concentrate hard on my balance. Can you get fined for being drunk in charge of a bike; I ponder?

Fortunately, the A2 is quiet and as the high winds of the previous day have now abated, the first couple of miles out of Carnlough make for easy cycling as I follow the coastline northwards. Away up to my left the nine glens of Antrim seem to stretch ever upwards in emerald-green swathes. My concentration is broken when a car immediately behind me blares its horn. Glancing over my shoulder I see the driver waving for me to pull over by the roadside. My first thoughts were that's it's an undercover police car and that I'm about to be breathalysed. It turns out to be Mr Aiken waving my wallet out of the window – I've only just gone and left my wallet at the B&B.

'I think ye will be needin this,' he shouts with a smile.

Purple with embarrassment, I thank him profusely, wave goodbye and cycle on with a great sense of relief.

Half an hour later and the A2 sweeps left at Garron Point where Red Bay opens up. The Bay was so named many years ago because the sandstone washed down into the sea by the many mountain streams in the area turned the beach red.

I make my first brief stop of the day in the small villages of Glenariff and Waterfoot. It seems strange that it should have a choice of two names but that indeed is what it said on the sign as I cycle into Glenariff, a mere 600 yards from Waterfoot.

The two villages nestle snugly in the crook of the bay at the foot of the River Glenariff as it enters the sea. Stopping on a narrow bridge over the river gives me with the ideal opportunity to take a photograph of one of Antrim's famous glens.

Two demanding inclines later and I am cycling into Cushendall, a town situated at the bottom of Glen Ballyeamon. Flicking down through the gears, the road starts to ascend once again quickly out of Cushendall when a sign catches my eye – 'Cushendall Concrete Garden Ornaments'. The sight of more concrete garden ornaments than you can ever imagine in one place, just warrants investigation.

The road up to the workshop is lined with concrete gnomes, soldiers, angels, birds, and more animals than even Noah would have seen. Propping my bike against a wall, I wander inside this concrete maternity hospital where one of the midwives is busy taping up the fingers of both hands with electrician's tape.

'Nice morning, do you mind if I have a look around,' I say cheerily.

'Sure, nae problem we get lots of visitors,' he replies.

The midwife's name is John, and we chat away about the moulding process involved in making concrete garden ornaments?

'Why are you taping your fingers John?'

'If I don't, I'll rip the skin aff me fingers whan I peel the rubber moulds from the cast. First the rubber mould must be cleaned by hand with detergent and left to dry after ejecting its previous occupant, then it is sandwiched between two sections of fibreglass, moulded exactly to fit, and special clips then joining the two sections together. Concrete is poured into the mould through a hole in the bottom. The whole thing is then left to set for 24 hours

or more depending on the temperature and finally the outside fibreglass mould is removed, and the rubber mould peeled from the concrete ornament,' he adds.

I watch intently as John proceeds to remove the outside glass fibre mould from a 3-foot-high angel and then to peel away the rubber mould with great dexterity. He has immensely strong fingers, no doubt developed by days and days of peeling moulds from ornaments. John tells me that the company supply garden centres and shops all over Europe and they can turn out up to 100 ornaments a day.

Declining John's offer of a 'free sample' to take away with me, I set off again up the steep slope out of Cushendall on the A2 Tromra Road towards its twin sister Cushendun. Approaching Cushendun I have a decision to make, do I follow the coast road up towards Torr Head or head direct along the A2 towards Ballycastle. Having driven up the coast road some years ago, I remember that it has some incredibly steep ascents and after the hard day I had yesterday and the excesses of last night, I decide to forgo the delights of one of the most scenic routes in Ireland and opt for the easier more direct route up the A2.

So much for the easy option – the next six miles are horrendous. The ascents are the steepest and longest I have encountered on the trip so far, in particular the long slow drag up towards the Ballypatrick Forest. On the plus side, by now any remnants of my hangover have completely disappeared.

When the road levels out, it's a great sense of relief to flick back up through the gears at the vanishing lake', or Loughareema as it is officially called, just on the edge of the forest. My guidebook informs me that this is an ephemeral lake (ephemeral lakes and ponds are basins that remain flooded for short periods of time during a year but may not hold water for several years if the rainfall regime is not suitable to produce flooding.) The lake seems to have vanished today as there is no sign of water, just a dried-up brown and green mud bed on either side of the road.

Stopping briefly by the non-existent lake, I get my first sight of Torr Head away to my right. It stands out starkly against the midday sun with the mountains of the Mull of Kintyre poking upwards just across the Irish sea beyond. Torr Head is the closest Ireland ever gets to Scotland, a mere 13 miles as the crow flies – little wonder the Irish had (and still do have) an affinity to the Scots.

Freewheeling the last couple of miles downhill, through the village of Ballyvoy and into the picturesque little harbour town of Ballycastle, my stomach begins to rumble. A quick glance at my watch tells me my stomach isn't lying – it is indeed lunchtime.

An attractive little town of some 4,000 inhabitants, Ballycastle sits on the shores of a wide unsheltered bay where the Atlantic Ocean meets the Irish Sea at the foot of the Knocklayde Mountain (more of a hill really at 1,500 feet high).

My memories of Ballycastle as a youngster are vague, but I do remember a day trip there to see the famous Ould Lammas Fair. A ballad written by local shopkeeper and bog-oak carver John Henry MacAuley enhanced the local fame of the fair. His song has stuck in my mind ever since:

Oh, the Ould Lammas Fair, boys, were you ever there?
Were you ever at the fair at Ballycastle-O?
Did you treat your Mary Ann to dulce and yellow man?
At the Ould Lammas Fair at Ballycastle-O

The fair, held every year on the last Monday and Tuesday of August, has been running for nearly 400 years. Its gastronomic specialities, as mentioned in the song, are 'Dulce' and 'Yellow Man'. Dulce is a type of dried, salted edible seaweed and Yellow Man is a sort of cinder toffee, both eaten in vast quantities during the week of the festival. Yellowman or yellaman is a chewy, toffee-textured honeycomb, a bit like cinder toffee.

I can remember trying both these delicacies all those years ago, and whilst the Dulse made me retch, I enjoyed the sickly-sweet taste of the Yellow Man.

In 1898, Guglielmo Marconi set up the first ever wireless link in the world across from Ballycastle to Rathlin Island, eight miles out in the Irish Sea. Born in Bologna Italy on 25 April 1874, Marconi, at the age of twenty-two moved to London where he was offered a contract by Lloyd's to set up a wireless link between Ballycastle and Rathlin Island. At that time Rathlin was an important point off the Irish coast, as all shipping from America and Canada passed its lighthouse en route for Liverpool, Glasgow or Belfast. The lighthouse keepers kept a record of all ships passing, but as it took a long time to get this information to London, a link to the mainland was important.

Five years later in 1901, Marconi sent the first trans-Atlantic wireless signal from Cornwall to Newfoundland, a distance of 1,800 miles, a feat that was to set him on his way to earning the Nobel prize for Physics in 1909. A large rock to his memory was erected on the top of the cliffs by the citizens of Ballycastle overlooking the harbour.

With lunch now on my agenda, I opt for the Strand Restaurant near the harbour. Not the cheapest lunch for a cyclist on a budget, but it is delicious, and I have the pleasure of chatting to an American couple over on holiday in Ireland. As seems to be the norm, they are astonished that I am undertaking such an onerous trip and wish me well.

Suitably refreshed, I take the B15 out of Ballycastle where I stop for a few minutes at the headland to read the plaque erected to Marconi and to admire the view across to Rathlin Island.

Rathlin Island, or Raghery as it was called in ancient times, has been inhabited for 8,000 years and is the last inhabited island off the coast of Northern Ireland with a population of just over a hundred hardy souls. Contrast this

with a hundred years ago when more than 1,000 people scratched out a living on this bleak and spartan piece of land just five miles by three. Treacherous currents that run between the island and the mainland have been responsible for many maritime tragedies over the years.

Thackeray, on his trips around Ireland in 1846, wisely decided to give Rathlin Island a miss as he said that the sea *'looked decidedly rough and treacherous'*.

The island, home to vast colonies of breeding sea birds including Manx Shearwaters and Fulmar Petrels, attracts visitors from all over the world. This small speck of land, shaped like a boot with the toe pointing towards Ballycastle, was at the centre of a territorial argument during the Middle Ages when the ownership of this rather bleak piece of real estate was disputed between Ireland and Scotland. The dispute was finally settled in Ireland's favour in 1617 after a celebrated court case, on the grounds that there were no snakes on the island.

Rathlin Island is probably the only place in the province of Ulster to have been unaffected by the troubles and was popular for people wanting to get away from the 'marching season' each summer during the late 70s and 80s.

Cycling on westwards along the north Antrim coast on the B15, I pass a sign for the Carrick-a-Rede Rope Bridge. A popular tourist attraction that links

the mainland to Carrick-a-Rede Island, the bridge was built in 1755 by salmon fishermen to link the mainland to this bleak chunk of rock.

With a target of fifty to sixty miles a day, I don't have time to visit the bridge today and with another eighteen miles to cycle, I press on along the North Antrim coast.

A few minutes later and I'm cycling past the small single-track road leading down to the quaint little harbour village of Ballintoy. The B15 coast road is popular for tourists, and has numerous lay-bys, at one of them I have the good fortune to stumble across an artist called Bill Yeaman.

Stopping for a drink, I wander over to where Bill is sitting by his battered old dormobile near the cliff edge with his paints and easel. A freelance artist from Newtownards, Bill spends his summers near his holiday home painting dramatic views of the North Antrim coastline and selling them.

Bill gives me the usual Irish greeting: 'How ye doin bye, ye look knackered', with a broad grin on his face.

'It's been a long haul up from Cushendun. How long have you been painting on this coastline?' I ask.

'A gud few years now, since I retired – sure it's a beautiful coastline is it not?'

Bill then takes great delight in pointing out his holiday cottage on the far side of White Park Bay and shows me his collections of paintings. One in particular catches my eye and despite the load in my carriers I ask Bill how much it is.

'Och sure if you like it you can heve it free of charge,' he replies, despite my offer to pay.

Thanking Bill profusely, I wave him goodbye and cycle on towards one of the eighth wonders of the world and Ireland's most famous tourist attractions, the Giant's Causeway.

Turning off the A2 on to the B146, aptly named Causeway Road, I pass Dunseverick Castle, a castle that was an important ancient site in Ireland dating back to the 16th century. Saint Patrick is recorded as having visited the castle in the 5th century AD, where he baptized Olcán, a local man who later became a Bishop of Ireland. The original stone fort that occupied the position was attacked by Viking raiders in 870 AD. At present all that remains of Dunseverick Castle are wall fragments of a tower and some overgrown foundations on top of the promontory.

Four miles of easy cycling later and I'm passing the entrance to the Causeway. Made up of some 37,000 perfectly formed hexagonal pillars of basalt (although some have seven or even eight sides), the Giant's Causeway is one of Ireland's most photographed landmarks. According to legend, Scottish giant Finn Mac Cool built the causeway so that his fellow Scots could step over from Scotland to attack the Irish, a theory made even more realistic by similar columns on the island of Staffa, in the Hebrides just across the Irish Sea. In reality, a huge volcanic eruption that occurred sixty million years ago formed the pillars.

Thackeray summed up the causeway in 1832 when he wrote:

'Mon Dieu! And I have travelled 150 miles to see that.
It looks like the beginning of the world.'

The B146 now turns inland at the entrance to the Causeway, and I soon link up with the A2 again a mile north of the village of Bushmills. By now my legs are beginning to feel the effects of the day's cycling and the gentle descent down into Bushmills is most welcome. If the name 'Bushmills' rings a bell with you, it's probably because you like a drop of the auld Irish whiskey. The Irish were pioneers in the development of distilling whiskey and the connoisseurs amongst you will already have made the connexion. Bushmills is the home of the oldest licensed distillery in the world, whiskey having been distilled here since 1608 when Sir Thomas Phillips was granted a licence to distil; in fact, the earliest mention of distilling in the town goes even further back to 1276. My father often used to enjoy a glass or three of Bushmills leading offering – Black Bush, the 'Rolls Royce' of whiskeys he used to call it. As I coast down into the town smoke from the famous distillery wafts its intoxicating fumes into my nostrils.

As the day is starting to 'wear on', I make tracks out of Bushmills and cycle on towards holiday resort of Portrush. Stopping for a few minutes rest at the ruins of Dunluce Castle I marvel at its location on an isolated rock stack separated from the mainland by a deep chasm. Built by Richard de Burg, Earl of Ulster at the end of the fourteenth century, the castle is one of the most picturesque ruins in Ireland, standing precariously on a rocky buttress some 20 feet from the cliff edge. It is said than in 1639 the kitchens of the castle collapsed into the sea during a raging storm, taking with them all but one of the servants who were busily preparing a grand feast. Thackery wrote of Dunluce Castle when he visited the area in 1843:

> *Those Grey towers of Dunluce standing upon a leaden rock and looking as if some old princess of old fairy times were dragon guarded within.*

My legs are now feeling the effects of the hard day in the saddle and my mind turns towards a comfortable room, a shower, a pint of Guinness and some hot food as I cross into my sixth County of the trip, Londonderry. With over forty miles under my wheels since leaving Carnlough, Portrush, just a mere four miles of easy cycling ahead of me, is my target for an overnight stop. One of Ulster's main seaside towns, Portrush attracts hordes of day-trippers from Belfast and other towns each summer and is sure to be lively in late June. Passing the Royal Portrush Golf club, I make a last-minute decision however, to give Portrush's ice cream and candyfloss a miss and head on another four miles towards its little brother Portstewart.

The A2 from Portrush to Portstewart is part of the world-famous North-West 200 motorcycle race route, one of only two public road races still permitted in the UK (the Isle of Man TT being the other). The NW 200 is synonymous with one of Ulster's greatest sporting sons – Joey Dunlop MBE OBE, a legend in County Antrim. Dunlop tragically lost his life whilst racing in Estonia during the summer of 2000, but his record in motorbike racing is legendary – five world titles, twenty-three Isle of Man wins, twelve NW 200 wins and countless other victories during his illustrious career. Fifty thousand people turned up to pay their respects at Dunlop's funeral in July 2000, bringing North Antrim to a virtual standstill, a poignant demonstration of the affection felt in this part of the world towards their Ulster hero.

As I cycle along one of the three legs of the course towards Portstewart my mind drifts back to the 1950s when my dad took me to motorcycle races around the province. I can almost smell the heady fumes of those two-stroke Hondas, Suzukis and Ducatis, the high-pitched screams of the 125s and the deep throated roar of the 500s as they hurtled along this very road. For a moment I'm Joey Dunlop and wave to the crowds perched along the roadsides – one can always dream.

Portstewart, with a population of around 8,000, is a beautiful, picturesque little town tucked is neatly into a bay of golden sands some two miles long, its little sheltered harbour protected from the prevailing northerly winds by a rocky outcrop. A much quieter town than its brash big brother Portrush, it was a popular watering place for the Victorian middle-class families during the 18th and 19th centuries when the Stewart family owned most of the area around the town.

Most towns in Ireland have famous residents and Portstewart's is Harry Gregg. Gregg is one of Ulster's most famous footballers, having played for Manchester United and Northern Ireland in the early 1960s. He was once the proud owner of the Windsor Hotel overlooking the harbour, a name dedicated to the legendary Windsor Park, the international football ground in Belfast where he played many of his matches for Northern Ireland. Gregg was one of the lucky survivors from the much-documented Munich Air disaster in 1958 when so many of the Manchester United Busby Babes were killed.

By now exhaustion is kicking in and as I approach the town centre, a sign outside the Cul-Erg Guest House that is displaying vacancies catches my eye. A man is up a ladder at the front of the property repainting the front as I pull up at the gate.

Assuming he is the owner I shout up, 'can I book a room for the night?'

Climbing down the ladder he cheerfully tells me that they have a room available and to take my bike round the back into their yard.

The Cul-Erg is owned by Joe and Ann Maguire and a few minutes later I'm relaxing over a cup of tea in the lounge with them. The Maguires are a lovely couple and make me feel most welcome. After the usual ritual of a shower and a nap, I set off on foot to find a decent pub and somewhere to eat.

It is a mere five minutes-walk from the Cul Erg into Portstewart, and as I stroll along the promenade, the sun is setting across the bay. After a delicious meal in the Anchorage Inn, I wander back to the Cul Erg, day five is over and all is well with the world – tomorrow London/Derry calls.

Day's statistics: 47.6 miles – Average speed – 15.2mph – Time taken – 5hours 10 minutes – Max speed – 18.5mph

Chapter 9

Day 6 – Portstewart to Londonderry/Derry (45 miles)

It's now day six and I'm down bright and early in the Cul-Erg dining room for breakfast. As he serves me another one of those fantastic Ulster fries comprising a huge plateful of bacon, sausage, egg, tomatoes and a soda farl, Joe asks me:

'Where are hoping to get to today, Cecil?'

'Not too sure Joe, but hopefully Derry. My schedule is flexible, so it all depends on how I'm feeling and what the weather is like.'

'Good luck anyway for the rest of your trip,' he adds as he heads back to the kitchen.

It's a dull and misty morning when I wave goodbye to the Maguires and set off along the A2 towards Coleraine. Away to my right I can clearly see the village of Castlerock, a mere four miles as the crow flies across the mouth of the Bann River, a village that I will shortly pass through on my way along the coast. Unfortunately, other than swimming, there is no way of crossing the Bann until I get to Coleraine, five miles away, and then another five back to Castlerock.

The first couple of miles out of Portstewart are uphill, but as I'm still fresh as a daisy they are mere gentle inclines after yesterday's harsh climbs up to Ballycastle.

The A2 hugs the east bank of the River Bann and it's quite frustrating that I will be cycling back along the west bank when I reach Coleraine.

The first bridge over the river is right in the middle of the town and soon I'm negotiating the heavy morning traffic through the centre of Ulster's fourth biggest town.

Coleraine has a long history dating back to 5935 BC and is reputed to have some of the earliest evidence of human settlement in Ireland.

The town got its name when St Patrick arrived in the area and built a church on a spot next to the river Bann that was overgrown with ferns. Some local boys were burning the ferns, and this led to the area being called Cúil Raithin or nook of ferns. This was later anglicised as Colrain, Colerain and Coleraine.

The most direct route from Coleraine to London/Derry is the B201 through Limavady, but I opt for the more scenic but slightly longer route on the A2 along the coast.

Just past the village of Articlave I decide to take a small detour down into the seaside village of Castlerock for my mid-morning drink and snack. The earlier mist has now disappeared, and the sun is starting to show its face, as I freewheel down the steep hill into the centre of the village. Castlerock is famous for its ices, so a poke is called for, its consumption made even more delicious by the views across the sand dunes as the waves sweep in onto the wide sandy beach.

Remounting, I embark on the steep climb back up out of Castlerock and re-join the A2, where a few minutes later I'm the passing National Trust property of Downhill Demesne and Mussenden Temple.

A mansion built on the site in the late eighteenth century for Frederick, 4th Earl of Bristol and Lord Bishop of Derry, much of the building was destroyed by fire in 1851 before being rebuilt in the 1870s. It fell into disrepair after the Second World War before being refurbished by the National Trust in 1980.

The road begins to fall away beneath my wheels and I'm descending at the most alarming rate of knots towards the small hamlet of Downhill. As this is one of the steepest descents on my trip so far, I'm concentrating so much on keeping the bike upright that I only catch glimpse the ruins of Mussenden temple on the top of a hill to my right. Built in 1785 by Bishop Hervey of Derry, the temple perches precariously on a 120ft cliff top, high above the Atlantic Ocean, offering spectacular views westwards over Downhill Strand towards Magilligan Point and County Donegal.

The road levels out shortly after Downhill, and I coast along admiring the beautiful sandy beaches away to my right and the green wooded hillsides up to my left. Magilligan Point, four miles away stretches out into the Atlantic at the entrance to Lough Foyle, with the Republic of Ireland a mere half a mile across the water.

This small triangle of land was the site for one of Ulster's infamous prisons, opened in 1972 when the 'Troubles' in Ulster began to escalate. It quite easy to see why the site for the prison was chosen - a flat spur of land with little habitation, guarded on one side by the Foyle estuary and the other by the Atlantic, made it an excellent location.

During the eighteenth century, one of the most unusual horse races in Ireland took place annually on Magilligan sands when Church of Ireland clergymen challenged their Presbyterian counterparts to a race, with the winners keeping the year's parish tithes from both churches.

Shortly after the village of Glebe, overlooked by the 384 metre Binevenagh hill with its dramatic tree-lined escarpment, I turn off the A2 and onto the narrow and twisting B69 Sea Coast Road and cycle over the river Roe and through the village of Crindle.

Half an hour later I link up with the A2 again a mile or so outside the market town of Limavady, a town that developed from a small Plantation settlement founded by Sir Thomas Phillips. In 1610 Phillips was granted 13,100 acres of land in which he built the town.

Cycling on along the A2 towards Londonderry/Derry I discover that I'm on one of the busiest roads that I have encountered so far on my trip, cars and lorries whizz pass me inches away from my right shoulder.

Trying to ignore the traffic and with seventeen miles left to cycle, I put my head down and head on through the village of Ballykelly and past Shackleton Barracks, a former British Army camp that was opened in June 1971 at the height of the Troubles. During Operation Demetrius, between 1971 and 1972, this camp operated as an interrogation centre for the mass arrest and internment of 342 people suspected of being involved with IRA activities. The camp stands empty now, with its rows of identical houses standing in parallel lines with a military precision.

With my overnight stop now only about fifteen miles away, I cycle on through the villages of Greysteel and Eglinton and on towards Londonderry/Derry.

Approaching the outskirts of the city, I follow the signs for the Foyle Bridge. (When I made my trip Londonderry/Derry had only two bridges spanning the river, the Foyle and the Craigavon, before the Peace Bridge, a cycle and foot bridge, was opened in 2011).

Stopping for a few minutes at the apex of the bridge and with the late afternoon sun glistening off the river, I admire the spectacular views over Northern Ireland's second city. Sitting comfortably astride the Foyle, its row after of row of houses rise up in steep tiers from the water's edge. From my vantage point at the top of the bridge, I can make out the Craigavon bridge two miles upriver, a bridge that was built in 1933 and named after Northern Ireland's first Prime Minister at that time, Lord Craigavon.

Now a very popular tourist destination, Londonderry/Derry is perhaps one of the most interesting cities in the whole of Ireland. Set atop a hill in a most dramatic setting, it is bounded on the southeast by the Sperrin Mountains, on the north-west by the Donegal Mountains and to the east by the River Foyle.

The city's long history dates to the sixth century, when St Columba, a native of Donegal, founded his first abbey on a tree-crowned hill overlooking the river. With the steepest main street in Ireland, it is one of the finest examples in Europe of a medieval walled city to be built in western Europe.

One event stands out above all others during Londonderry/Derry's rich and turbulent history.

On 7 December 1688, thirteen apprentices locked the huge city gates to keep out James II's invading Jacobite regiment, and act of defiance by the youngsters that led to a siege lasting fifteen weeks, during which around 15,000 people died of starvation.

A second attempt began four months later, on 18 April 1689, when James himself appeared before the walls with an Irish army led by Jacobite and French officers, but this also failed when ships bringing food broke through to the town three months later.

The name Derry rather than Londonderry is preferred by nationalists, and it is broadly used throughout Northern Ireland's Catholic community, but many Unionists still prefer to call it Londonderry. In 1983 the City Council changed the name of the city from Londonderry to Derry. It has now been given the nickname of 'stroke city' by many people in Northern Ireland.

William Bulfin himself summed Derry up beautifully when he visited in 1907:

> *If Derry started life with a cool temper is has never cooled down. It has been something of a storm centre all through the ages. And it is a storm centre today. You cannot look upon it without a quickening of the pulses. Something of its rugged history speaks to you out of its quaint old streets. It sits there squarely astride the Foyle under wild Innishowen, the weatherbeaten citadel of the fighting North.*
>
> William Bulfin, *Rambles in Eirinn* 1907

Day's statistics: 45.00 miles – Average speed – 8.9mph – Time taken – 5hours 28 minutes – Max speed – 29.9mph

□

Chapter 10

Day 7 – Londonderry/Derry to Donegall Town (49 miles)

Leaving my comfortable little B&B near the city centre, I head for the Foyleside cycleway, part of the Sustrans National Cycle Network linking Londonderry/Derry to the border towns of Lifford and Strabane. The cycleway runs parallel to the A40 Foyle Road between the disused Foyle Valley railway line and the river.

The surface is excellent, and I fairly skim along on the north side of the Foyle. Passing under the rusting girders of the Craigavon Bridge, the morning sun is reflecting on the shimmering calm water on my left.

With a third of my trip almost complete, I will soon be leaving Northern Ireland and crossing the border again back into the Republic.

Soon I'm turn off the cycleway onto the Balloughry Road where I cross the border again into County Donegal and the Republic – the 7th County of my trip.

Expecting to see a modern building with smart uniformed guards, I'm somewhat disappointed when I pass a small flimsy sign perched precariously on the grass bank 'Stop Garda' it reads almost apologetically. A small decrepit portacabin, perched on the roadside with 'Mr. Garda' himself, fast asleep in a deckchair outside, sleeves rolled up and tie unfastened.

I'm ready to pull out my passport and to be grilled about the purpose of my trip, but as I approach, he doesn't even stir from his slumbers. There is something wonderfully Irish about this relaxed border crossing and I debate with myself as to whether I should just cycle on but thinking better of it I decide to stop. Rolling slowly up to the sleeping Garda, I call out, 'Excuse me but do I need to stop'. He sits bolt upright nearly jumping out of his skin but remains sitting in his chair.

'Ah you're ok, sure it's a brave day now, on ye go', he says casually as he settles back into his deckchair. Quite what purpose he is serving on this small country road miles from anywhere, I do not know, but it's a lovely morning to have a sleep in the sunshine.

Giving the border guard a quick wave, I cycle on back into the Republic of Ireland again. This relaxed attitude to the border crossing is in stark contrast to those days in the 1950s and 60s when you were required to stop at the first of two barriers – the Northern Ireland border post and then again about 100 yards later at the Republic border post – a most bizarre experience as I recall from my youth. Our car was usually thoroughly searched, and of course on the way back the process was reversed – it was an altogether irritating and time-consuming experience.

Even earlier, during the 1920s and 30s, travellers crossing into the North of Ireland from the South by car had to leave a deposit of a third of the value of their vehicle with the customs officers, to be reclaimed later when they crossed back. At that time cars were considerably more expensive in the North and many people made a living out of cross border car smuggling, often using the small, unmarked back roads, like the one I'm cycling along today. Bus passengers were also thoroughly searched with people having to alight from the bus to have their bags and parcels opened and searched by the customs officers before proceeding on their way. Such was the price differential between the two countries at the time that many people travelled north to buy new clothes and shoes, and on the way back left their old clothes and shoes in hedges just before reaching the border – it could only happen in Ireland.

Donegal, whilst the most northernly county in Ireland, is in the province of Ulster, a fact that causes much confusion. Ulster is made up of nine counties, Down, Antrim, Londonderry, Armagh, Fermanagh, Tyrone, Donegal, Cavan and Monaghan, whilst Northern Ireland has only the first six. To confuse things further, the original six counties planted with British settlers by James I in the early seventeenth century were Donegal, Londonderry, Armagh, Cavan, Tyrone and Fermanagh.

In 1912 when partition came on the agenda in Ireland, it was agreed that all nine of Ulster's counties would be split off from the Dublin Government, but four years later in 1916, Edward Carson and Lloyd George agreed that a six-county statelet would be the best option, primarily to ensure a Protestant majority in the north-east of the country.

Even the local accent in Donegal bears a much closer resemblance to the six counties of Northern Ireland than to the rest of the Republic, with many shops and filling stations near the border displaying their prices in both Punts and Sterling. Enough of this Irish history for the moment and back to my trip.

Cycling on along the R236 south-eastwards towards Donegal Town, I pass through the small towns of Raphoe, Convoy and Stranorlar before joining the N15 near Ballyboffey. Shortly after cycling through the picturesque Meenglass Forest, I pass Lough Mourne where the road begins to rise again rather steeply, and I have to drop down through the gears. It's now mid-afternoon and I'm struggling up the steep climb towards the Barnsmore Gap where, on reaching summit, I collapse in a heap on a grassy bank.

The views on either side of the gap are superb, the hills rise steeply to 1,000 feet on either side of high boggy gorges. Standing out starkly in the late afternoon sunshine, the rounded summits of the Blue Stack Mountains dominate Lough Eske on one side, whilst on the other side, the Barnesmore hills sweep away towards the border a mere two miles distant across the Barnsmore Bog. The river Eske winds its way down towards the town of Donegal some eight miles below.

Remounting, I off again on the final section down into Donegal town. It feels great to be freewheeling down the other side of the pass on the best road surface of the trip so far, and with only about seven miles left to cycle before I reach Donegal Town, I have no intention of stopping again. When the road begins to level out, a huge sign – 'Biddy O' Barnes Famous Pub' – catches my eye, why this pub in the middle of nowhere is so famous just has to be a subject for research so I coast into the large car park. Maybe it is the thought of half a of Guinness towards the end of a tiring day that sways the decision.

Settling back in the afternoon sunshine outside Biddy's Famous Pub with a half of the black stuff in my hand, I try to find out why this pub is so famous. The barmaid tells me that Biddy's was originally an Inn, dating back to the eighteenth century and with the coach at that time being the main form of transport, the Inn was a stopping point where the horses were rested, and travellers relaxed, before the next stage of their long and tiring journey through the Barnesmore Gap.

After a hard day in the saddle, the Guinness tastes good, and the location is stunning as I gaze across towards the blue waters of Lough Eske glistening in the late afternoon sunshine. With Donegal town in sight, I reluctantly drain my glass and set off again down the N15.

Reaching the outskirts of Donegal town, I come off the N15 and onto the R267 where a few years earlier my wife and I, along with a couple of friends, spent one night in a very nice B&B on the Old Laughey Road. I decide to check if they have a room available and when I knock on the door, I'm immediately recognised by John the owner.

'I'm very sorry but w're fully booked tonight,' he says apologetically, and noticing the look of disappointment on my face he continues, 'but some friends of ours have a B&B on the other side of the town and I'll give them a ring if you like.'

I wait patiently at the door as John makes the phone call and when he comes back a minute or so later, he tells me that 'Susannah's got a room available, and I'll take you over there if you like? Pop your bike in the back of the car.' A few minutes later and I'm unloading my bike from the boot of John's car, and after thanking him for his help I settle into Ballinderg House, the beautiful home of Susannah and Pat Hawthorn.

The Ballinderg, with it's large-manicured gardens sweeping down to the water's edge, is in a stunning location on the edge of Donegal Bay. From the window of my beautifully furnished room at the end of day six, I watch the evening sun sinking over Donegal Bay and Atlantic Ocean beyond.

The County town was established many centuries ago by the Vikings, before becoming the stronghold of the O'Donnell clan for nearly 400 years until the flight of the Earl of Tyrconnell in 1607. It was then granted to Sir Basil Brooke who in 1610 set about developing the centre into a triangular diamond adjacent to the ancient castle at the heart of the town.

It's only a five-minute walk from the Ballinderg into Donegal town centre and I'm heartened to find that every third building is either a pub or a restaurant. Spoilt for choice settle for a small, homely looking establishment called Murphy's Bar overlooking the Eske. It's still early evening when I enter, and only a couple of locals are there chatting to two German tourists at the bar when I order my pint. Whilst waiting for it to settle, another customer enters and greets the barman cheerily.

'Ow's it gannin' Declan?' he says in a broad Northeast of England accent. My wife is from that area and having spent some time there, I'm acutely aware of the local dialects and greet him with a wave.

'What part of the Northeast are you from?' I ask.

'Wy Sun'lan' man, de ye kna it'? he answers cheerfully.

'I know it well, I went to college and taught in a school there.' I respond. Peter and I get on like the proverbial 'house on fire' and we chat away about Wearside, the Durham coalfields, and the fortunes of our beloved Sunderland Football Club.

'Are you over in Donegal on holiday, Peter'? I ask.

'No Cecil, I live here noo. Aboot five years ago I came ower on holiday and liked it soo much I just stayed and gat a job as a winda cleaner. I clean aal the pub winda's in Donegal Town,' he says.

'Good job mate, I guess you get a free pint in each of them.' I reply with a grin.

A couple of pints of Guinness go down in no time whilst we reminisce about Sunderland football club. Peter offers to buy me another, but with visions of another alcoholic evening like the one in Carnlough three days previously, I decline gracefully if somewhat reluctantly, take my leave, bid goodbye to Peter and Declan and head back up into the town.

Strolling up through the Diamond looking for food, I catch sight of a sign that says, 'Donegal's World-Famous Chippy'. If this is a world-famous chippy then its delights just must be sampled by this hungry pedaller on his way round Ireland. After popping the first piece of fish and a few chips into my mouth I know that I have made the right decision – they are truly delicious. The claim that it is a 'word famous chippy' is indeed a worthy one.

It's a lovely evening as I stroll leisurely back down through the town centre happily munching my fish and chips from a paper bag. This is the life, a couple of pints of Guinness followed by fish and chips in a quiet Irish town on a beautiful summer's evening. Not the ideal food for a serious athlete on a marathon cycle ride of course, but they are delicious and of course tomorrow's ride is still twelve hours away anyway.

The one thing you can always guarantee about Ireland is that the weather can change within a matter of minutes, and as I make my way back to the Ballinderg, the glorious sunshine of the last few hours suddenly turns to rain. It begins to pour down in torrents, and I'm forced to take shelter in a shop doorway. After finishing my supper, and with the rain showing little sign of easing, I contemplate making a dash for the Ballinderg, but as often happens in Ireland, it stops raining as quickly as it started leaving one of those beautiful cool moist Irish June evenings where everything smells so fresh – a great end to the first week of my trip.

Day's statistics: 61.6 miles – Average speed – 10.3mph – Time taken – 4hours 22 minutes – Max speed – 26.6mph

Chapter 11

Day 8 – Donegal Town to Strandhill (51 miles)

It's now day eight, I wave goodbye to the Hawthorns and set off out of Donegal town along the east shore of the Bay on the R267. Three miles later after a steep incline, I join the N15 where the road levels out and I'm able to enjoy the luxury of a steady downhill section through the village of Laghy.

Shortly after passing Durnesh Lough, I cycle through the Rossnowlagh crossroads, into Coolmore and on towards Ballyshannon, a town that straddles the River Erne. Guarding what was in earlier centuries an important strategic crossing point over the river, Ballyshannon dates to 1500BC. It's Abbey Mill Bridge, built by the Cistercian monks, is reputedly the oldest bridge in Ireland.

William Allingham, one of Ireland's most famous poets, was born in Ballyshannon on 19 March 1824 a hometown that inspired some of his best-known works – Adieu to Ballyshanny, The Fairies, Laurence Bloomfield in Ireland.

In his poem Adieu to Ballyshanny he wrote of the town:

> *An odd out of the way little town, ours. On the extreme western edge of Europe, our next neighbour's sunset way, being citizens of the great new republic which, to our imagination seemed little, if at all, farther off than England in the opposite direction.*

Leaving Ballyshannon, I cycle on south westwards along the N15 towards Bundoran. The most southerly town in County Donegal, Bundoran, with excellent views across Donegal Bay to Saint John's Point, Muckross Head and Slieve League, is one of the most popular seaside resorts in Ireland. Popular with surfers, it has been listed by National Geographic magazine as one of the World's Top 20 Surf Towns.

Tourism has been at the heart of its local economy since the eighteenth century, and astonishingly, with a population of less than 2,000, it has one third of the total number of gaming machines in Ireland. This is an incredible statistic for a small town – perhaps it should be twinned with Las Vegas.

Resisting the temptation to try my luck on the machines in Mack's amusements, I bypass the town and cycle on along the N15 towards Sligo. A few minutes later and I'm entering the eighth county of my trip – Leitrim. With the shortest coastline of any county in Ireland, just 2½ miles long, I'm soon leaving Leitrim and into my ninth – Sligo.

The N15 is as straight as an arrow and soon I'm flying along through the townland of Castlegal where over to my right, I can just make out the outline of the peninsula of Mullaghmore with its impressive lighthouse. It was just outside Mullaghmore harbour where the IRA assassinated Earl Mountbatten of Burma in 1979 whilst out on a fishing trip with his family. Mountbatten's holiday home, Classiebawn Castle, a Victorian Baronial building sits on the cliffs like Dracula's lair overlooking the bay. The Castle was built for the then British Prime Minister Lord Palmerston in the late 19th Century.

A bomb planted onboard Mountbatten's small fishing boat cut short his life at the age of seventy-nine. His teenage grandson, Nicholas Knatchbull and a local teenager, Paul Maxwell also died in the tragedy. It was an event that did little to improve Anglo-Irish relations at a time when tensions between the two countries were running high.

Zipping on through the village of Cliffony, the north-eastern tip of the Streedagh peninsula appears over to my right, with the broad expanse of the Strand glistening in the afternoon sunshine. Known as Spanish country, this part of Sligo 'entertained' the Spanish Armada when it was making a dash for home after its abortive assault on the English in 1588. Three ships were grounded near Streedagh Strand after 1,800 Spanish sailors perished when their wooden ships broke up like matchsticks when a south westerly gale smashed them onto the rocky promontories. Just over 100 survived and were able to make it ashore.

The fortunate Spaniards who survived the sinkings faced suspicious locals, some of whom murdered them in a most cruel fashion, whilst others subjected them to overwhelming Irish hospitality. One particular survivor, Captain Francisco de Cuellar, managed to crawl ashore on Streedagh Strand and, despite the hostility of the Sligo people, was able to make it back to his native Spain.

A year or so later in a letter to a friend, he recounted his adventures in Sligo:

> *On the fifth day there sprang up a great storm on our beam, with a sea up to the heavens, so that the cables could not hold, nor the sails serve us, and we were driven ashore.... The shore were full of enemies, who went about jumping and dancing with delight at our misfortunes; and when any one of our people reached beach, two hundred savages and other enemies fell upon him and stripped him of what he had on until he was left in his naked skin.*

At Grange the road swings due south and towering away to my left, the huge, rounded hill of limestone that is Benbulbin, is silhouetted in the afternoon sunshine. A striking outcrop of rock some 1,500 feet high, it dominates the surrounding landscape with its sheer face dropping away almost vertically to the lush green fields below. Benbulbin is a protected site, designated as a County Geological Site by Sligo County Council.

Half an hour later and I'm cycling through the village of Drumcliff, where I'm left in no doubt that I'm now in Yeats country. A Yeats tavern, a Yeats restaurant and a Yeats hotel, gives the game away. William Butler Yeats, an Irish poet and one of the foremost figures of twentieth century literature, was born in Sandymount near Dublin. He spent childhood holidays in County Sligo where he fell in love with the county.

Yeats was one of those poets whose work was forced down my throat during those interminably boring poetry lessons at school. Sorry Miss Gibson (Mrs Rea) if you happen to be reading this.

Just south of the village a signpost catches my eye, 'Drumcliff Church Grave of W.B. Yeats.'

Turning off the main road, I cycle down a narrow single-track road to the church and stop by his graveside. Yeats' grave is a simple affair with a headstone bearing the immortal words from his poem Under Benbulbin:

Cast a cold eye On life, on death. Horseman, pass by!

An epitaph that he wrote for himself, and, according to his careful directions.

Yeats lived a large portion of his life in the South of France. He died there in 1939, and his ashes were buried in a pauper's grave near Monaco, where they remained until 1948 when they were dug up and brought back here to Drumcliff in his native Sligo. The Sligo locals said at the time that they brought back the wrong remains and that Yeats is not buried here at all – but who is to know for certain? Drumcliffe has made the most of their famous son though, with tourists flocking to the area each year to pay their respects to the great man.

Benbulbin looms over the church and it obviously made a huge impact on Yeats as he left a legacy to the hill in one of his most famous poems.

Under bare Ben Bulbin's head
In Drumcliffe Churchyard Yeats is laid.
An ancestor was rector there
Long years ago, a church stands near,
By the road an ancient cross.
No marble, no connectional phrase;
On limestone quarried near the spot by his command these words are cut.
Cast a cold eye
On life, or death.
Horseman, pass by!

After spending a few moments at the graveside, I cycle back down the narrow road, onto the N15 and on southwards.

Half and an hour later I'm cycling into Sligo town. With a population of around 20,000, Sligo straddles the Garavogue River where it runs into the bay of the same name. The town lies in a beautiful setting surrounded on three sides by an arc of mountains.

Even though by now I'm feeling the effects of a hard day in the saddle, I decide to cycle on a further six miles towards the small seaside resort of Strandhill.

On a late June Sunday afternoon, Strandhill is buzzing. The sea front is alive with families enjoying the beautiful clean white sand and clear blue sea. Cafés, bars and ice cream kiosks are doing a roaring trade, whilst surfers are riding the huge waves that sweep in from the Atlantic. With a population of just 650, Strandhill more than triples during the weekends when visitors from Sligo descend on it.

Whilst pints of the black stuff being consumed outside the bars looks appealing, finding a B&B is top of my agenda after a long day in saddle. Cycling along the sea front, most of the B&Bs have 'no vacancy' signs hanging outside, and I begin to wonder whether I will have to cycle back into Sligo after all. Fortunately, the Mardel, just next to the golf course has a 'vacancy' sign and I gladly accept the offer of a room from the landlady Anne Marie Kelly.

After parking my bike in the garage at the rear, I slump wearily into a chair in the comfortable lounge, gratefully accepting Anne Marie's offer of a cup of tea and a cake. Waiting for my tea to arrive, I spot a copy of Tony Hawks book 'Round Ireland With A Fridge' on the coffee table.

When Anne Marie brings me my tea and cake, I point to the book. 'It was this that motivated me to undertake this cycle trip round Ireland.' I tell her.

'He stayed here when he visited Strandhill and you're in the same room as he had.' She replies with a smile.

Well, you could have knocked me over with a feather, what are the odds of me stumbling on the same guest house that Hawks stayed in and being given the same room?

Anne Marie and I chat away about Hawks book and his visit to the village seven years previously and she tells me: 'He embellished some of the details in the book just a little, but it's true though that he did take the fridge surfing off the beach just across the road and got somewhat inebriated in the Strand pub afterwards.'

After settling into my room and changing, I stroll along the sea front towards the Strand pub for my obligatory evening pint of the black stuff, if the Strand is good enough for Hawkes, then it's good enough for me.

The sun is sinking fast out over the Atlantic, courting couples are canoodling on the sea wall and children are playing on the sandy beach whilst their parents sit watching from the wall quaffing pint. It's a wonderful setting at the end of day eight, with just over a third of my trip completed and a pint in my hand, I sit on the sea wall gazing out over the blue Atlantic.

A large glass-fronted building catches my eye. On first glance, it looks like the front of what you would expect from a tourist office, but the sign over the entrance says otherwise – 'Celtic Seaweed Baths'.

Draining my pint, my curiosity gets the better of me and I stroll over to look. Entering the spotlessly clean reception area a young chap behind the desk greets me with the usual Irish charm and friendliness.

'Good evening sur, we're closing shortly but I can book you in for tomorrow morning if you like,' he says.

'I'm cycling around Ireland, and I will be leaving fairly early. What time do you open'?

'Fair play to you now sur, (I'm becoming familiar with this well used Irish phrase 'fair play to you', which roughly translated means 'well done or 'good on you') we open at nine in the morning, sure a bath will set you on your way, it's great for relaxing the muscles,' he responds.

The young man greeting me is none other than the joint owner of the baths and he is called Neil. A former Irish international triathlete, Neil goes on to tell me that: 'The coastline around Sligo abounds with a particular type of seaweed that, when soaked in hot seawater, releases rich and silky essential oils. The health benefits of seaweed have been well documented for some time, there is seaweed skin cream, seaweed shampoo and many other seaweed-based products on sale in health shops. The oils make your body feel smooth, buoyant, and luxurious, tiredness, tension, aches and pains just slip away, the skin is re-hydrated and moisturised whilst conditions such as

Psoriasis, acne and dry skin can be eased. It can also aid back and muscular pains, rheumatism and assist circulation.'

Never having had a seaweed bath before I've just got to give this a try, so I book a session for nine the next morning. With my muscles aching from the last seven days hard cycling, perhaps this is just the sort of pampering my body needs.

With food now high on my list of priorities, I stroll across to the Strand again hoping to get a meal. Unfortunately, they don't do food on a Sunday evening, but the barman is helpful:

'Try the Ocean View Hotel, it's about a twenty-minute walk up the hill but the food is excellent and very reasonable,' he tells me.

I decide to give the Ocean View a try and I set off walking up the steep hill out of the village. By the time I reach the hotel it's a welcome relief to sink into one of the comfy chairs in the bar lounge.

The views back over Strandhill and the Atlantic beyond are well worth the trek alone, as is the superb bar meal I devour in double quick time. Fortunately, the walk back to the Mardel is downhill and twenty minutes later, after resisting the temptation to pop into the Strand for a nightcap, I roll into bed completely exhausted at the end of another tiring but rewarding day.

Day's statistics: 51.4 miles – Average speed – 8.6mph – Time taken – 5hours 58 minutes – Max speed – 27.9mph

Chapter 12

Day 9 – Strandhill to Knock (50 miles)

After another of those excellent full Irish breakfasts, I walk the fifty yards or so from the Mardel to the Celtic seaweed baths where Neil is waiting to greet me.

'Have a seat for a minute now and we'll soon have you rockin and rollin,' he says cheerfully.

A few minutes later he shows me into a beautifully clean tiled cubicle that contains a traditional metal bath and a steam cabin.

'You need to spend five minutes in the steam cubicle and then soak in the bath for about 10 minutes, then repeat the process up to four times depending how you feel. The steam opens the pores of the skin and allows the full benefit of the seaweed to penetrate the body,' he tells me.

It's a strange feeling lowering myself into a bath filled with what can only be described as brown/green slime. Gazing down into the bath, my only concern is that all the creepy crawly creatures you normally find on the seashore have been removed from this batch, as I don't fancy my private parts nipped by a baby crab.

Settling back into the warm silky mixture, it feels quite wonderful, and within minutes my skin is feeling smooth and silky and the stiffness in my leg muscles begins to ease.

Lying back enjoying the warm seawater and rubbing the seaweed all over my body, I ponder whether I might be able to take a photograph to prove that I have indeed taken this seaweed experience. I think of calling Neil back in to take one, but perhaps that might just be a tad embarrassing, so I opt to balance my camera on the door handle, set the auto timer and hopefully be back in the bath before it goes off. The results are much better than I could have hoped for, more by luck than good judgement.

With my body positively glowing after my seaweed bath, I set off out of Strandhill on the morning of day nine. The climb up out of the town on the Buenos Ayres Drive towards the R292 is quite gentle, and with a light breeze at my back it's an easy start the day.

Buenos Ayres Drive – now there is a road name to conjure with. What, you may wonder, is the connection between this Irish coastal town and the capital of Argentina? At the beginning of the twentieth century, Strandhill was an empty landscape of sandbanks, a far cry from the pretty seaside destination of today.

The answer has nothing to do with either fine wine or warm weather, but apparently a man called Murrow purchased land in the area in 1877 and named the functional route from the village to the seaside Buenos Ayres Drive, inspired by the Argentinean capital, albeit spelt differently. Why he had desire to commemorate the Latin American city we don't know but suffice to say it adds a continental feel to the coastal town.

Very soon I'm cycling past the 1,000 feet high huge outcrop of rock called Knocknarea (In Gaelic Ard na riaghadh, the hill of the executions.) A stone cairn on its summit top marks the grave of Queen Maeve (or Medhbh as she was called). Maeve was the ancient mystical Queen of Connacht, who according to legend, was a malevolent queen who could make men go quite mad. The cairn is a huge flat-topped mound of stones, 34 feet high and 600 feet in circumference and contains a passage grave.

The view from the summit of this impressive hill is said to be quite superb with fine views of Sligo town, Drumcliffe Bay, Ballysadare Bay and of course Sligo Bay itself, but with a full day's cycling ahead I resist the temptation to make my way to top.

Leaving Knocknarea behind, I cycle on along the east shore of Ballysadare Bay, passing through the village of Belladrihid, and soon I'm cycling into the town of Ballysadare itself. A quiet, respectful, sober little town for most of the year, Ballysadare comes alive for one week in the year when its annual pop festival attracts the youth from all over the world for a jamboree of music, singing and dancing. There is no sign of pop groups or groups of any kind on this sunny day in June though as I cycle through.

It is at this point that I have another decision to make, do I head directly south towards Galway or head west into County Mayo towards Ballina, Castlebar and around the coast? To go around by Mayo and the Connemara National Park is a tempting prospect, but as it will put an extra 100 miles and two more days onto my journey, I decide to head south towards Galway.

Half an hour later I am cycling past the Slieveward bog into the town of Coolaney, where I stop for a few minutes on the bridge over the Owenmore River. During the 19th Century, Coolaney was an important trading post, when the river was the lifeblood for the dark imposing satanic mills built on its banks.

The town's most notable citizen was a man called Bryan Higgins, a man who rose to fame in 1779 when he invented cement. Higgins obtained a patent for a cheap and durable product made up of sand and lime with a proportion of bone-ash. He slaked the mixture with limewater instead of common water, and hence cement was born in this small village in Ireland.

Just south of Coolaney I join the N17 and head on southwest, through the towns of Ballynacarrow, Tubbercurry and Charlestown where I enter county number ten of my trip – Mayo.

Two hours of hard cycling later and with fifty miles under my tyres since leaving Strandhill, I arrive in Knock.

At the southern end of the main street almost every house is displaying a B&B sign with most indicating that they have vacancies. Spoilt for choice I opt for Raffertys, a nice-looking detached house set just back from the main road in its own grounds.

Mrs Rafferty herself answers my ring on the doorbell, and it is evident that she is somewhat taken aback when she sees this sweaty Lycra clad 'apparition' standing in front of her. As I find out later, her usual clientele are sober pilgrims rather than round Ireland cyclists.

'Have you got a room for one night?' I enquire politely.

'I surely do, would you like to see it,' she says.

'No need Mrs Rafferty, I'm sure it will be fine, is there somewhere I can leave my bike it where it will be safe?'

'Sure, ye can chain it to the trektor, rund the bak, it'll be safe ther', she indicates with her thumb.

My mind conjures up a vision of me chasing this 'trektor' round the fields the next morning with my bike dragging along behind it, but as if reading my mind Mrs Rafferty adds:

'Ah sure the trektor hasn't moved for thirty years.'

Chaining my bike to this rusting hulk at the back of the house, I'm quite confident that this 'trektor' will never plough the green fields of County Mayo again and that unless someone has a 'thing' about stealing rusty pieces of farm machinery, then my bike will be safe.

After settling into my comfortable but rather dated room, I shower the day's road dust off my tired body and stroll up the main street towards the Shrine, or the Basilica Complex as it is known. There are very few people around and what strikes me immediately is the sense of peace and tranquillity in the air. Although I'm not a Catholic, there is an aura about the place that makes the hairs on the back of my neck stand on end, I even feel uncomfortable taking a few photos of the holy place.

With a population of only around 500, at certain times of the year, Knock's population expands tenfold to as many as 5,000, but on this quiet June evening it is very quiet.

This little town of Knock shot to world prominence on a wet Thursday evening in August 1879, when at around 8pm, Our Lady, St Joseph and St John reputedly appeared in a blaze of heavenly light at the south gable of Father Cavanagh's parish church. Two local people were convinced that they had witnessed this apparition and summoned thirteen others to verify the miracle. The church authorities accepted their account of the happening and ever since then pilgrims have flocked to Knock in their droves to pay homage to the Saints.

The Catholic Church has held the town of Knock in such high esteem that in 1957 it was affiliated to the Basilica of St Mary Major in Rome with special privileges granted to pilgrims. Pope John-Paul II paid a visit to the town on the centenary of the apparition in 1979 when he endorsed the indelible seal of Vatican approval. At the rear of the chapel, set in a glass case, is a very impressive large golden rose that he presented during his visit.

Knock Basilica is the largest church in Ireland with a capacity of 12,000, and with an International Airport nearby, pilgrims can fly in for the day, pay their homage and be back home in time for supper.

Sitting on a bench opposite the huge glass windows, I'm somewhat puzzled by what looks like a row of drinking fountains. Some people are filling up plastic water bottles whilst others are dabbing their foreheads with the water and suddenly dawns on me that these are self-service holy water fountains.

The centrepiece of the shrine is an original stone from the old church of 1879 set into the gable end of the chapel where a queue of people is filing past, kissing the stone, and blessing themselves.

Strolling down the main street in the early evening I'm surprised that Knock is so quiet, most of the shops are shut apart from a tacky little market selling souvenirs. On the lookout for my pre-dinner pint, I'm struggling to find a pub. The only one seems to Coleman's Bar, so I pop in. I'm the only customer and with no chance of a chat with any of the locals, I quickly drain my glass and head on down to the outskirts of the town, where I have the good fortune to stumble upon Carty's Bar. With several upmarket cars parked outside it certainly seems busy. Wating for my pint to be poured, I strike up a conversation at the bar with a man called Pat. A Belfast man by birth, Pat worked overseas for many years before returning to Ireland and buying a B&B just outside Knock.

'Pity I didn't know about your place Pat; I've just booked into Mrs Raffertys.'

'Ah sure you'll be great there Cecil, she is a lovely lady.'

Expressing my surprise about the lack of pubs in the town Pat explains:

'Cher this is the ony dacent wan. I don't think the church encourages the drink as it puts the pilgrims aff,' he says with a twinkle in his eye.

Day's statistics: 49.3 miles – Average speed – 9.5mph – Time taken – 5hours 09 minutes – Max speed – 26.6mph

Chapter 13

Day 10 – Knock to Maam Cross (53 Miles)

After another delicious full Irish breakfast, I leave Knock to the pilgrims and head on south-west along the busy N17. The traffic whizzes past me at a rate of knots and it is a welcome relief to turn onto the much quieter R331 towards Ballinrobe at Claremorris.

My plan for today is to cycle to the north shore of Galway Bay somewhere near Rossaveal, a ride of around fifty miles. Tomorrow I intend to take a ferry out to the Aran Islands and my research informed me that Rossaveal is the gateway to the Aran Islands.

Twenty minutes later and I'm cycling into Ballinrobe, the largest town in south Mayo. Stopping for a mid-morning drink and a snack near the superb Catholic Church of St Mary, I admire its beautiful stained-glass windows by Harry Clark, one of Ireland's most famous stained-glass artists.

It is from this part of County Mayo that the often-used word 'boycott' originates. Entering the English language during the Irish Land Wars that began in 1879, the word takes its name from Captain Charles Cunningham Boycott, the land agent for an absentee landlord Lord Erne. Thirty-eight small tenant farmers rented land on Lord Erne's estates and Boycott was very strict with them, showing no leniency when rents were in arrears, and restricted their movements.

The local population, led by Father O'Malley went on strike and refused to lift Boycott's potato crop and thrash his corn. Boycotting proved to be an extremely effective tactic, and the Land League went from strength to strength.

From Ballinrobe I cycle on directly due south, through the village of Neale, and soon reach the town of Cong where I stop for my lunchtime sandwich and drink.

With a population of around 200, Cong is a delightful little town sitting on an island in the middle of a river by the same name. Its name evolved from the Irish word 'cunga'.

Cycling into the village, I'm surprised how busy it is, but I soon learn why when I stop on a lovely wooden bench outside the tourist office and consult my guidebook.

If you are a film buff or a John Wayne fan, you will know why this small, out of the way village in County Mayo, is so busy in late June. Cong was one of the main locations for the filming in 1951 of John Ford's classic movie *The Quiet Man*, starring Wayne and Maureen O'Hara.

Cong certainly doesn't let you forget the fact that it played host to 'yer man' big John Wayne, the whole town seems to be themed around the film. After finishing my snack, I wander around the town and begin to get 'Quiet-Man-itis' (just made that up). There is a Quiet Man pub, a Quiet Man coffee bar, a Quiet Man hostel and of course a Quiet Man Heritage Centre based on a replica of a 1920s 'white-o-mornin' cottage with its thatched roof, emerald-green half door and whitewashed front that features in the film. There is even a shop in the main street selling black and white photos of scenes from the film.

A quick browse round the leaflets in the tourist office and I realise that Cong has other historic attractions way back before big John arrived in the town. Its Abbey, dating back to the seventh century, was destroyed by fire in the early twelfth century before Turlough O'Connor, the High King of Ireland re-built it in 1135. Very little remains of the Abbey today except for the cloister, where the monks once worked and prayed, along with the north doorway and several other elaborate doorways that open onto the cloisters from the east range. Since then, a new church has been built to the rear: a weathered concrete monstrosity that looks to me totally out of place on such an historic site.

Cycling out of Cong and passing over the Cong dry canal, I enter the eleventh county of my trip, Galway.

The Cong canal was built in the late 1800s as a famine relief scheme, to provide employment for the local people. It was an attempt to link the two adjacent Loughs, Mask and Corrib, but after taking five years to build when water was released into the newly completed canal, it immediately vanished. The ground underneath was porous limestone much to the dismay of the engineer when he saw his beloved project literally 'vanish down the plughole.' Sounds like one of those Irish jokes does it not?

A couple of miles out of Cong I pass Ashford Castle. The castle was built on the perimeter of a monastic site in 1228 by the Anglo-Norman House of Burke. Rebuilt in the nineteenth century by the Guinness family, it is now a luxury hotel and was used as a set for the *Quiet Man* film in 1951. Three miles later and I'm re-joining the R345 where it runs alongside the tranquil waters of Lough Corrib towards the small village of Cornamona. The countryside now begins to take on a more rugged and barren appearance as the road twists and turns along the shoreline. Out in the Lough to my left a multitude of small, heavily wooded islands dot the clear blue waters.

Approaching the village of Cornamona, I skid to an abrupt halt outside a general store. I'm not hungry or thirsty, but the name above the door catches my eye – Lowrys. Thinking that perhaps I might have relations in this part of County Galway, I pop inside and ask the lady behind the counter: 'Are you Mrs Lowry'?

'No, I'm not, I just work in the shop. Mr Lowry is the owner, but he is away today,' she replies.

'My name is also Lowry and I just wondered if maybe we were in any way related?'

'You would need to pop back tomorrow and ask him.'

Of course, as that is out of the question, I jump back into the saddle and press on south-westwards.

At the village of Maum I leave the R345 and swing south on the R336, where in the distance away to my right, I get my first glimpse of the jagged peaks of the mountains. Pointing like fingers into the blue sky, the Maumturk mountain dominates the Connemara National Park. The Connemara National Park was founded and opened to the public in 1980 and features 2,000 hectares of mountains, bogs, heaths, grasslands, and forests. The Partry

Mountains and the 673-metre-high peak of Maumtrasna rise dramatically away in the distance.

I'm now in Joyce country, a region that takes its name from James Joyce's ancestors who settled in the area in the thirteenth century. Joyce was an Irish novelist, short story writer, poet, teacher, and literary critic, contributed to the modernist avant-garde movement, and is regarded as one of the most influential and important writers of the twentieth century.

Having covered around forty miles since leaving Knock, and now feeling quite tired, I stop to examine my map. As mentioned earlier, I've set my sights on the village of Rossaveal on the north shore of Galway Bay, but as it's another twenty miles away, so my only option seems to be the village of Maam Cross, a mere five-mile cycle along the R336.

Remounting wearily, I drop the bike down into bottom gear and soon I'm climbing steadily up the Maam valley between Lackavrea Mountain on my left and Maumwee on my right. Whilst the scenery is stunning, it's a mighty effort to turn the pedals over as the road goes interminably upwards. Low black clouds envelope the surrounding peaks and the threat of rain does not seem too far away.

On reaching the summit of the pass, I breathe a sigh of relief and as if by magic the clouds disappear, and a brilliant late afternoon sun lights up the superb vista down towards Galway Bay. I can just make out the distant shapes of the four Aran Islands, one of which I hope to visit tomorrow.

The last few miles of the day into Maam Cross are downhill and I'm able to admire the bleak but beautiful peat bogs of Connemara as I coast along. On both sides of the road, long symmetrical trenches stretch away into the distance, reminding me of First World War battlefields. Alongside the trenches blocks of peat glisten in the sun as they dry out. A couple of months previously the turf would have been cut into slabs about a yard long and piled in mounds by squads of labourers using a slean (a long thin type of spade.) The slabs of wet turf are then left to dry over the summer months and collected in the autumn. This annual ritual of cutting of turf has been an essential part of Irish life in this part of the country since time immemorial, providing employment for thousands of people.

Soon after passing Manwee Lough and Lough Hanillaun, I cycle into the little hamlet of Maam Cross where I hope to find accommodation for the night. All I can see is a hotel, a petrol station, and a cluster of houses - not a B&B in sight.

The hotel is called Peacockes, and will probably be a bit over my budget, but I'm so tired by now that I'm going to book a room regardless of the price. Another fifteen miles of cycling down to Rossaveal just does not bear thinking about and there will be no guarantee that I will find a B & B. The only other alternative is to cycle another twenty miles into Galway city, but of course I will then have to cycle another twenty miles back out to Rossaveel tomorrow morning, so Peacockes it is.

Chaining my bike to a handrail near the entrance and feeling somewhat conspicuous in my cycling gear I clatter into reception. The lounge bar is filled with business reps and American tourists, and this sweaty, dishevelled person in Lycra shorts and t-shirt, lugging a pair of panniers and a rucksack feels totally out of place.

The receptionist doesn't even raise an eyebrow when I enquire if they have a room available.

'No problem sir, we can give you an en suite room at fifty punts including full Irish breakfast,' she says.

Without a second thought I readily accept, register, and make my way up to my room on the first floor.

Peacockes Hotel in Maam Cross is excellent: my room is spacious, has satellite TV, telephone, and a huge bath – the bath is probably worth the extra twenty-five punts above what I have normally been paying anyway. There is nothing better after a hard day's cycling than to soak in a hot soapy bath, only the second time on the trip since the farm McCann on day two.Whilst my bath is running, I relax on the huge comfortable double bed and watch the news on the TV. The main story is the effects of the foot and mouth outbreak a couple of months earlier that devastated the Irish cattle stock and the forthcoming move to adopt the Euro in Ireland.

On returning to the bathroom, I'm horrified to see that my luxurious bathwater is a deep rust colour. Picking up the telephone I dial reception:

'This is room 213, the hot water in my room is coming out of the taps brown,' I inform the receptionist.

'Ah sure it's not a problem sur, all the water run this part of Ireland is brown, it's down to the peat bogs ye see. It's perfectly clean and you can drink it quite safely,' she says cheerily.

Half an hour later I'm still wallowing in a bathtub full of peat coloured water – to be honest it is so relaxing that I couldn't care if it was red, blue or green.

My usual routine of finding a local pub followed by a cheap and cheerful restaurant goes by the wayside in Maam Cross – because there just aren't any – it's a pint in the hotel bar and dinner in the adjoining restaurant tonight.

Supping my first pint of the day, I pick up a brochure that tells me a little about Maam Cross. The area is renowned for its October Fair where all manner of goods is sold, from ducks, hens and rabbits to donkeys, ponies and horses as well as the usual fair day stalls. I'm also surprised to discover that Maam Cross has a favourite son, a Scottish immigrant called Alexander Nimmo. Nimmo, the son of a Fife watchmaker who settled in the village in the early nineteenth century was responsible for transforming much of the infrastructure of Ireland during that time.

During his brief sojourn in Ireland, Nimmo was responsible for developing much of the west of the country including the road from Galway to Clifden on which Maam Cross sits. He also pioneered the railways in Ireland, designed and built a pier in Galway and developed the road link between Kerry and Cork. (I'm to come across more of Nimmo's work later on my trip).

Day's statistics: 52.5 miles – Average speed – 10.4mph – Time taken – 5hours 01 minutes – Max speed – 33.1mph

Chapter 14

Day 11 – Maam Cross to Lahinch (29 miles)

Day eleven dawns bright and sunny and an early start is required if I want to make it to Rossaveal for the 10.30am ferry to the Aran Island of Inisheer. I'm the first person into breakfast at six thirty, and by eight I'm loaded and on my way.

After an hour and a half of easy cycling along the R336 I'm coasting down into Rossaveal. With a local population of just over 1,000, this tiny hamlet on an estuary just off Galway Bay would be an insignificant place if it were not for the fact that it is one of the gateways to the Aran Islands. A smattering of houses, a couple of shops and the obligatory pub line both sides of the road leading down to the tiny harbour.

It would be a travesty if I did not take in one of Ireland's most famous island groups on this trip, so I decided at the planning stage to visit the most southerly island of Inisheer (Inis Oirr in Gaelic). The smallest of the three main Aran islands, it is the only one that has a ferry service that runs from Rossaveal and back to Doolin on the south shore of Galway Bay. It is a logical choice as I can then continue my trip south in County Clare.

Whilst more than 2,000 people a day visit the Aran Islands in the summer months, more than doubling their resident population, Rossaveal harbour is quiet when I arrive at the ticket office.

A group of school children are jostling noisily around their teacher, who is speaking loudly to them in Gaelic. This does not surprise me as this part of the west of Ireland is a bastion of the Gaelic language. The Aran Islands still maintain Gaelic as their native language with English as their second.

It was a beautiful morning when I left Maam Cross a half an hour earlier but standing on the quayside waiting to board the ferry, low threatening clouds are starting to sweep in from the Atlantic bringing with them a fine drizzle. The ferry crew are most helpful, and my bike is hoisted on board in a matter of seconds and secured on the upper deck.

As the ferry edges slowly out of the harbour, Inisheer is a mere blip on the horizon, looking much further away than the scheduled forty-minute trip. On clearing the harbour and entering the open Atlantic, the ferry picks up speed to around twenty knots (so a crew member told me) and in no time at all we are entering the small, sheltered harbour of Caherard.

My guidebook tells me that all three of the Aran Islands are crisscrossed with a series of more than thirteen miles of eight-foot-high drystone walls, each enclosing a small barren and rock-strewn field no bigger than an average back garden. Over the centuries, the islanders created fertile land by clearing rocks from a small area and piling them into walls, enclosing a small patch of ground.

A readily available mixture of seaweed and sand enabled them to grow potatoes, cabbages, and onions within these walled enclosures.

The Aran islanders lived a life of extraordinary hardship and poverty, collecting seaweed that was dried and burnt to make kelp (from which iodine is extracted) to supplement their diets and to sell to the mainlanders. Children were raised from their beds at all hours of the night to rush down to the seashore, where buckets and any other available vessels were filled with this precious natural product. It was thought at the time that kelp was given to the islanders by God. The wrack was spread out to dry on the stone walls from August until June each year when it would then be burnt in kilns to produce the valuable product. For every thirty tons of the wet seaweed collected, one ton of kelp would be produced – a very labour-intensive business.

By the mid-twentieth century, tourism began to change the way of life for the Aran islanders, as traditional farming gave way to hotels, bars, restaurants and B&Bs.

By the 1980s more than 10,000 people were visiting the three islands. The pressure of tourism began to cause conflicting views amongst the islanders, but the resulting boost to their economy was most welcome, and most accepted the changes.

Setting off from Caherard harbour in an anti-clockwise direction around the island, I fairly whizz along on a very narrow smooth tarmac road. There is no need to be on the lookout for vehicles as there are very few on Innisheer – the odd tractor perhaps.

Ten minutes later and the smooth tarmac turns into uneven slabs of limestone but with 540 miles under my saddle, and now a seasoned cyclist, I arrogantly weave my way in and out of the huge slabs. My trip nearly comes to an end when I hit a rock, almost throwing me over the handlebars. Shaken but not stirred, I carry at just about walking pace before deciding that the track is becoming too hazardous to continue, so I abandon the idea of circumnavigating the whole island and cut back inland towards the harbour.

Cycling gingerly between the 8ft high stone walls I realise that I'm lost. How can you get lost on a four-square mile island you may ask? The nearest explanation I can offer is that it feels like cycling around a giant maze, walls and paths twist and turn crazily in all directions and I begin to wonder if I'm destined to cycle round Innisheer for the rest of the day.

Dismounting, I climb one of the high walls to get some idea where the harbour is. The high walls have been providing me with shelter from the brisk south-westerly wind that is blowing in off the Atlantic, but as I peer above them, my cycling glasses are whipped off into the grassy bank.

Eventually I make it back to the only pub on the island near the harbour called O'Flaherty's, named after the O'Flaherty family from Connemara who captured the island in 1582. Lunch is called for at this point and over an excellent clam chowder, I chat to some American tourists who are visiting Ireland for the first time. They are astonished that I have my bike with me on the island and that I'm on a marathon round Ireland cycle trip.

Gazing up at the wide unobstructed skies and down to the mighty North Atlantic sweeping in over the jagged rocks below, it is not difficult to understand why tourists from all over the world flock to the Aran Islands in large numbers. There is softness in the air and an incredible charm about the place that once visited, you will never forget it – I know I certainly won't. Bidding my newfound American friends goodbye, I cycle back the few hundred yards down to the harbour to catch the ferry back to the mainland.

Innisheer is a mere six miles off the coast of county Clare and less than an hour later I'm cycling ashore at Doolin on the south shore of Galway Bay where I'm now entering the twelfth county of my trip - Clare.

The River Alle from the ferry terminal runs through the centre of Doolin before it pours into the Atlantic. as it wends its way towards the Atlantic. Doolin's claim to fame is that it is the birthplace of Micho Russell – who's he I hear you ask? Russell, a local farmer was a bit of a whiz on the old tin whistle and flute who came from a musically renowned family. He taught himself to play the tin whistle by ear starting at age eleven and in 1973, won the All-Ireland tin whistle competition. His knowledge of tradition extended past music to language, stories, dance, herbal lore, and old country cures. Clare has been the Mecca for traditional Irish music for centuries.

This part of Ireland is renowned as being a mystical place, and many visitors arrive looking for that magic 'something' which might change their lives. Apparently Doolin lies on the meeting of ley lines, lines that are supposed to create a 'buzz' in the air. I must admit that I'm unable to find any sort of buzz as I struggle up the hill from the harbour.

It's a steep climb up the R 459 towards Roadford where I swing directly south. Cycling along the colourful modern bungalows dotted randomly around the countryside, as if some giant had thrown confetti at a wedding are astonishing.

After the exertion of the particularly steep climb up from Doolin, I stop for a rest at the junction with the R478. From this vantage point, the views across to the Aran Islands and the entrance to Galway Bay are stupendous, their barren bleakness and beauty takes my breath away. Back over my shoulder to the east, the huge limestone plateau known as the Burren stretches away in the distance. Considered of such importance, the Irish Government is gradually establishing it as a National Park. (Since my trip, it's now an established National Park - the sixth smallest in Ireland).

John Betjeman neatly sums up this part of Ireland in his poem: Sunday in Ireland:

Stony seaboard, far and foreign,
Stony hills poured over space,
Stony outcrop of the Burren,

Stones in every fertile place,
Little fields with boulders d Grey-stone shoulders saffron-spotted,
Stone-walled cabins
Thatched with reeds,
Where a Stone Age people
The last of Europe's stone age race.

It's time to move on, and after a quick glance at my map, the holiday town of Lahinch about an hour's cycle away, seems like a reasonable target for my overnight stop.

After four miles of hard cycling along the R478 into a stiff breeze and squally showers, I arrive at one of Ireland's top tourist attractions, the Cliffs of Moher.

One of the big advantages of being on a bike is that you can just ignore 'no vehicular entry' signs and cycle right to the heart of the action – in this case the vantage points overlooking the stunning cliffs. Cycling up from the car and coach park, I glide effortlessly pass busloads of tourists making their way on foot.

With their highest point some 668ft above sea level and stretching along the Atlantic coast for about five miles, the cliffs look like a series of noses. There are six in total making it one of Ireland's most dramatic landscapes jutting out into the foaming Atlantic Ocean.

An attraction that attracts around half a million visitors a year, the cliffs were formed three hundred million years ago. It's a place where nature can be experienced in the raw, particularly when gales sweep in from the Atlantic.

Turning these stunning cliffs into a visitor attraction was the brainchild of Cornelius O' Brien in 1855. One of the wealthiest men in Ireland, O'Brien was the landlord of ten thousand acrest ts in Co Clare and a local Liberal MP. When he first opened the Cliffs, O'Brien hired a piper to play each day to entertain visitors. One day it was noticed that the sound of piping coming from the direction of the cliffs had suddenly stopped, and on investigation it was discovered that the piper had fallen over the cliffs. Locals said that he liked a drink and was often seen to be unsteady on his feet while he piped.

As a result of this, a six-foot high wall was built to prevent people falling over. Over the years, the wall has been reduced to a mere three feet as you can see from my photo.

Wheeling my bike along the narrow path along the top of the cliffs, I find the steep drop away into the ocean below quite dramatic. The views back across towards the three Aran Islands are unbelievably breath-taking. Sea bird's wheel and dive on the thermals above my head and far below boats bob in the ocean below.

A few hundred yards further up the path I come to O'Brien's Tower. Built in 1835 so that visitors could enjoy the views, it is now a café and souvenir shop selling a wide variety of Cliffs of Moher merchandise. They are charging a punt to walk up the stone staircase to the top of the tower, all of 30 feet, quite what you will be able to see from a further 30ft up at the top of the tower that you can't see from the bottom, I really don't know. Its late afternoon by now and having soaked up the views, I remount, leave the Cliffs behind and cycle on towards Liscannor Bay and Lahinch.

The earlier rain showers have now turned into a persistent drizzle, and with a stiff headwind, I make my way slowly southwards along the R478. Fifteen minutes later and the road swings at right angles eastwards at St Brigid's well. One of the oldest wells in Ireland and rumoured to have healing powers, it is housed in an open stone house or grotto that serves as a gateway to an ancient cemetery. According to my guidebook, the natural beauty, and the mysterious pull of the well makes it special in a land known for its roadside shrines and mysticism.

Ten minutes later and I'm cycling into the small fishing village of Liscannor on the northern shores of the Bay of the same name. Liscannor (Lios Ceannuir in Gaelic) was famous for the stone quarried from the rich seams of the Doonagore mines in the early 1900s. The mine became so prosperous in the early 1900s, that a village was built.

At that time Liscannor was one of the busiest of the small ports along the west coast of Ireland, its shipments of stone leaving for London and Liverpool daily.

With the outbreak of World War in 1914, boats were unable to sail, and the mines closed. Half a century later several mines were re-opened on a smaller scale in the Liscannor area and are still producing the famous stone today. Liscannor's most famous son is John Philip Holland. Born in the town in 1840, he emigrated to the USA in 1873 where he developed the first submarine to be formally commissioned by the US Navy.

Heading on east towards Lahinch, I cross over the Inagh River and into Lahinch, where for the first time on this trip, I'm struggling to find a B&B. The first three places I pass have 'no vacancies' signs, but eventually I find one down a side street just off Station Road.

After the obligatory shower and short nap, I set off the hundred yards or so down to the main street to look for a pub. Kenny's Bar on the main street catches my eye, so I pop in for a pint. It's still early evening and Kenny's is quiet when I perch myself on a stool by the bar and order my pint of the black stuff. As usual, I immediately strike up a conversation with a couple of locals who quiz me in depth about my trip and my reasons for undertaking what they think is a tough cycle. The barman also joins in the conversation and when my pint arrives, he will not hear of payment – 'It's on the house mate.' he says. 'You deserve a pint for undertaking such a trip.'

The barman turns out to be none other than mine host Kenny himself, and when I order my second pint, again he will not hear of payment. If I felt like it, I can stay drinking at the bar all evening on his tab, but after enjoying one of his delicious bar meals, I bid goodbye to Kenny and make my way back to my B&B. (I told Kenny that I would give his pub a mention, so if you are ever in Lahinch, call in for a drink and tell him I sent you.)

Strolling back up the main street, it would appear that Kenny is a well-known man in Lahinch. Looks like he owns half of it – as well as his bar there is a Kenny's gift shop, a Kenny's supermarket, and a Kenny's hotel – no wonder he can afford a few free pints to a wandering cyclist.

Lahinch, a traditional Irish seaside town with a population of around 700, has been been popular with visitors since the late 1800s mainly due to its excellent championship golf course. In July 1887, with the opening of the West Clare Railway, visitors flocked to the area and it has thrived ever since.

Lahinch was in turmoil during the troubles back in late September 1920, when many residents fled their homes and hid in the sand dunes around the bay to protect them from the Royal Irish Constabulary who were doing house to house searches. The RIC were seeking revenge for an ambush carried out by the IRA at Drummin Hill near the hamlet of Rineen three miles to the south, when they attacked a Royal Irish Constabulary lorry, killing six officers.

Day's statistics: 39.00 miles – Average speed – 10.2mph – Time taken – 3hours 36 minutes – Max speed – 31.5mph

Chapter 15

Day 12 – Lahinch to Listowel (44 miles)

I groan aloud when I part the curtains of my bedroom window on day twelve. It's one of those damp, drizzly Irish mornings, you know the sort of rain – that fine, soft rain that finds its way through to your skin – even through the best waterproof clothing. An uncomfortable day's ride is on the cards if this rain persists. Looking at my map, it dawns on me that I'm just about half-way through the trip. I feel quite emotional, but there is still a long way to go.

Lingering over breakfast with one eye out of the window, the local radio station at least gives me something to smile about. The newsreader is informing the good citizens of Clare about a five-year-old boy, who after having recently been taught to cycle by his father, had disappeared on his bike. 'The Garda launched a full-scale search and fortunately the young lad was found safe and well, having cycled eighteen miles from his home.' He announces. The significance of cycling this distance by a five-year old strikes a chord as I am only too aware of the effort and risks involved in cycling eighteen miles on Irish roads.

Loading my panniers onto their carrier, I notice that it has shed a small bolt causing it to wobble about. Whilst not vital, it needs to be replaced so I clip off my panniers and stroll down the main street to look for a shop that might sell bolts. There doesn't seem to be any hardware shops in Lahinch and the only possible place I can find is a small garage. The entrance is simply a hole in the wall wide enough to take one car, with space for a couple more inside. Walking into this dark deserted cavern the unmistakable smell of petrol and sawdust assault my olfactory senses.

'Hello anyone about' I shout.

A voice from somewhere in the deep recesses at the back of the garage replies: 'Aye come thru the bek bye.'

Carefully making my way through a maze of used rusty car parts, I find my way into a small back room that serves as an office, store and tea-room where a jolly faced gentleman is sipping tea from a huge, chipped pot and reading the morning paper. A old dusty radio is blaring out a rousing Irish reel.

'Would you have a small bolt for my bike?' I ask, showing him the pannier with the hole where the bolt should be.

'Sure I'll hev a luke fer ye,' he says, before proceeding to poke about in a series of little boxes from where in a matter of seconds, a bolt of just the right size appears as if by magic. 'Sure, let me pit in on fer ye,' he says, grabbing a spanner that is also exactly the right size.

'How much do I owe you', I say.

'Away we ye now, sure it's only a wee bolt,' he replies – again that Irish willingness to help a visitor.

Fortunately, the rain has abated, but there are still some threatening black clouds hovering just off the coast as I set off again at southwards.

The N67 runs along the south side of Liscannor Bay and after about forty-five minutes hard cycling into a stiff headwind, I eventually turn onto the quieter R482 towards Spanish Point. An elbow of land jutting out into the Atlantic, it is so named because many of the Spanish Armada ships were blown ashore onto its beaches in 1588 as they fled for home after their defeat in the English Channel.

Rejoining the N67 just a couple of miles south of the point, I cycle through the village of Quilty, onto the R483 and on through Creegh and Cooraclare.

The stiff south westerly that has been bugging me all morning is still blowing unpleasantly into my face, and to make matters worse it starts to rain again. After a quick sandwich at a filling station, I set off again in the drizzle towards the Shannon.

Dropping down the hill into Kilrush the rain abates, and I have a great view of the Shannon estuary. Whilst planning the trip, I had earmarked nine significant landmarks as I made my way around Ireland: crossing the border from the republic into the north, my hometown of Downpatrick, the Giant's

Causeway, crossing the border back again into the republic, the Aran Islands, crossing the River Shannon, the Lakes of Killarney, Cork and finally Dublin. Number six is now in my sights on day twelve.

Kilrush, with a population of just under 3,000 souls, is a bustling little town. Pretty pastel-coloured buildings dominate its centre. The 'Maid of Eireann' monument representing the 'Manchester Martyrs' sits in its impressive main street. The monument is dedicated to Philip Allen, Michael Larkin and Michael O'Brien, leaders of the Fenian movement in Manchester, who were executed in November 1867.

(A number of memorials were erected in Ireland to honour the memory of these three men.)

Negotiating the tricky one-way system through Kilrush proves somewhat of a challenge, but by now I'm an expert on Irish traffic behaviour and without incident, I soon re-join the N67 and head on towards the north shore of the Shannon estuary.

Half an hour later and I'm cycling through the village of Killimer where I have clear view of another one of those ugly monstrosities, they call power stations. Moneypoint is Ireland's largest power station providing around twenty-five per cent of the country's electricity needs and burns over two million tons of coal per year. Its disgusting dirty grey fingers point up into the clear blue sky, blighting the landscape along one of Europe's finest rivers.

Sticking to my plan of trying to avoid major cities, I intend to cross the Shannon on the ferry that runs between Killimer and Tarbert, thereby avoiding Limerick, Irelands third largest city. When I arrive in Killimer I find that the ferry has not yet left Tarbert, giving me twenty minutes or so to relax in the sunshine that has replaced the rain, after my efforts cycling into the wind down from Mohr.

Sipping a welcome cup of tea and devouring a cake outside a small café, a carload of noisy American tourists plonk themselves at an adjoining table. When a guitar is produced, I fear the worst, but the quality of the country and western songs they start singing is excellent and I enjoy the foot tapping tunes.

When the ferry pulls into the quayside, I bid farewell to the Yanks who pack away their guitars and call out to me 'take it easy now, good luck man'.

Crossing the Shannon from Killimer to Tarbert takes no more than twenty minutes and as the ferry approaches the headland, another of those ugly grey power stations casts its drab shadow over the estuary. This one looks as though it's nodding to its brother on the north of the river and saying, 'You spoil that side and I'll spoil this side.'

It's a beautiful clear day and Loop Head, County Clare's most southernmost point, is just visible twenty miles away in the distance at the entrance to the estuary. Loop Head lighthouse, originally a coal burning brazier on a platform on the roof of the cottage where the lightkeeper lived, has pointed the way for mariners entering and leaving the Shannon since 1670. The first 'tower' lighthouse built in 1802, it was replaced with a new tower in 1854, and in 1869 its light changed from being fixed to flashing.

Looking back up the Shannon towards Limerick, I can just make out the western tip of Foynes Island. An inconspicuous little piece of land, this island was significant during the Second World War when it was the original Shannon Airport. Whilst the Republic of Ireland was, in theory, neutral during World War II, most passengers through Foynes were top level Allied military and diplomatic personnel with the necessary high priority status required for transatlantic flights. Many were on active duty and travelling under false passports. At first the airlines were very circumspect about the identity of many of these passengers but as the war progressed more American military uniforms were seen. There is no doubt that, with the tacit approval of the Irish government, the flying boat base was a very important link in the Allied war effort. The old disused air terminal at Foynes now houses a flying boat museum displaying many of the original models, photographs, and logbooks from those wartime military operations.

Cycling off the ferry at Tarbert, I enter the fourteenth county of my trip – Kerry. Probably one of the most mystical and magical counties of Ireland, Kerry is the sort of place where you can expect something weird to pop up from behind a hill at any moment. The Irish believes in fairies, leprechauns, and other things not of this earth, and Kerry, perhaps more than any other county fits this stereotype.

It's now mid-afternoon, and as I cycle south along the N67 my legs are beginning to send signals to my brain, 'look pal, we've had enough down here so how about doing a deal and calling it a day?' they seem to be saying.

After a quick glance at the map, the town of Listowel about an hour's cycling away, seem like a good option for my overnight stop.

Half an hour later with a drink stop on my mind, I spot a sign near the village of Tarmon, 'Kissane's Candle Factory – Visitors Welcome.' I'm curious to find out why a candle factory is in the middle of nowhere, so I pull into the small car park next to a small, corrugated iron building. Ireland has always been famous for its cottage industries, and this is certainly one of them. There is no sign of life when I peer through the open door into the deserted workshop, until suddenly a man emerges from the house next to the workshop and greets me cheerfully.

'Hallo how ya,' he says with a big smile, 'I'm Joe Kissane.'

'Pleased to meet you Joe,' I reply. 'Just saw your sign and though I'd drop in for a look.'

'Sure, your most welcome. By you've got a powerful luggage on that bike,' he adds with a grin.

When I explain that I am cycling round Ireland he is even more enthusiastic.

'Come on in and have a wee look round the workshop, you get a drink whilst I tell you how it's done,' he says.

Joe tells me that he started making candles in his garage as a hobby a few years previously, and when they proved popular with friends and relatives, he decided to build a unit on the land to the rear and set up as a small business. His main market is making candles for special occasions, such as weddings, christenings, and anniversaries, some of the candles on display in his small showroom are truly works of art and it would seem a shame to burn them.

Joe explains that most candles today have fragrances added to the wax, and for nearly an hour he painstakingly outlines the procedure. He insists that I smell all the special scents he puts in his candles, with his own favourite being vanilla and coconut.

'When I'm making vanilla and coconut candles, I always imagine I'm sitting on a Caribbean beach drinking Malibu' he says with a laugh. Closing my eyes and smelling one I can understand where he is coming from.

In today's high-powered, big business cut-throat world, it is a pleasure to spend an hour with a man who is obviously passionate about his job. Bidding Joe farewell and declining his kind offer of a free candle, I set off again to cycle the last ten miles into Listowel.

With a population of almost 5,000, and one of the larger towns in this part of Kerry, it should not be difficult to find a decent B&B in the heritage market town of Listowel. Whilst there a few B & Bs in the town centre, all of them are displaying 'No Vacancies' signs and I spend twenty fruitless minutes cycling around the town centre. Stopping at a small shop, I enquire as to where I'm likely to find a somewhere to stay and am directed towards the Cahirdown district about a half a mile out of town back along the N69 where I stumble upon Liz and Peter Adams B & B.

After being made most welcome by the couple with a cup of tea and cake, I settle into my very spacious and comfortable room and take the opportunity of finding out a bit about Listowel from my guidebook.

Straddling the banks of the River Feale, Listowel (the fort of King Tuathal), has a long literary reputation. Designated a writer's town, in June every year it plays host to an annual Writers' Week when it celebrates many of its famous playwrights, poets, novelists, scholars and actors. Some of the best storytellers in Ireland originate from Listowel, (perhaps the abundance of pubs has something to do with it?).

On a more sombre note, the Town's Garden of Europe contains Ireland's only public monument to the memory of the millions who died in the Holocaust and to all victims of injustice and oppression. The bust of poet and philosopher Friedrich Schiller, a key figure in Germany's romantic movement, stands proudly in the gardens, a gift to Listowel from the German people. Carved in stone is a verse from Schiller's famous composition *'Ode to Joy.'*

I was surprised to learn that Listowel is twinned with my hometown of Downpatrick. (It's also twinned with Los Gatos California, Shawnee Kansas and Panissières, France.) Listowel is also home to Ireland's famous butter – Kerrygold, founded in 1972. I was amused to learn that some years later, a 35-year-old man had covered himself in butter to make it difficult for the Garda to arrest him, after barricading himself into his house in Listowel – could only happen in Ireland.

Listowel has been declared the drinking capital of Ireland with thirty-seven pubs serving a population of 3,500, apparently, there used to be fifty-two, but as demand dropped a few closed down. *(Ten years after I cycled through Listowel, a publican was prosecuted after the Garda police found dozens of nuns were found drinking illegally, several hours past closing time on his premises. Could only happen in Ireland.)*

Wandering on down the main street in search of a pint of the black stuff, a sign in the window of Flanagan's Bar catches my eye: 'Appearing tonight – The Batchelors'.

Those of you who grew up during the 1960s and 70s may well remember Con, Dec and John as one of Ireland's most popular singing groups? They were certainly one of my mother's favourite groups. Popping in for a pint I enquire of the barman what time the boys are appearing.

'They start their act about 10pm, but they are a tribute group, not the originals,' he tells me with a grin on his face, realising that I think they are the originals.

Suitably embarrassed, I sup my pint and decline the offer of another late night. The Batchelors will just have 'to see me in my dreams'. If you are too young, google it.

Day's statistics: 43.7 miles – Average speed – 8.3mph – Time taken – 5hours 13 minutes – Max speed – 29mph

Chapter 16

Day 13 – Listowel to Killarney (40 miles)

Having cycled exactly 611 miles since leaving Dun Laoghaire, I'm now just over halfway through my trip and it should be all downhill from now on – figuratively speaking of course.

Day thirteen dawns bright but somewhat blustery in Listowel. Leaving the warm hospitality of the Adams family I cycle out of the town, over the River Feale and on south-eastwards along the N69.

Fortunately, the blustery wind is blowing from the north-west helping me on my way, as I cycle through Mountcoal Cross, Banemore and Leampreaghane Cross towards Tralee.

The views of the Stacks and Glanaruddery mountains away to my left are stunning whilst the Slieve Mish Mountains dominate the landscape just to the south-east. Further along the peninsula to the west, I can just make out Mount Brandon before the land sweeps away towards the Dingle and Great Blasket Island.

Tralee is the county town of Kerry and has a population of around 18,000, more than double its more famous neighbour, Killarney. A popular gateway for travellers on their way to the lakes during the nineteenth century, Tralee is situated at the eastern end of the bay of the same name. The town is synonymous with its famous festival, the Rose of Tralee, a traditional beauty contest that is been held in the town every August for many years. Entrants must be female, have an Irish connexion (whatever that may be) and be able to compete not just on looks but also on personality, intelligence and something described as 'the truth ever dawning.' Whatever that means?

The Rose of Tralee festival is one of the most important events in the Irish social calendar, second only to St Patrick's Day for its colour, fervour and popularity, attracting a huge influx of visitors to the town during the third week in August each year. A vast amount of drink is consumed during the week and when the Rose is eventually crowned, the partygoers are usually in no fit state to appreciate the qualities of the winner.

I have Killarney in my sights for an overnight stop, so I cycle on out Tralee along the N70 towards Killorglin.

Crossing the River Maine at Castlemaine, I pedal on through Milltown and into Killorglin where I stop for a sandwich.

Browsing my guidebook on the bank of the River Laune, I discover that Killorglin is the venue for the 'Puck Fair' every August. One of only three great fairs left in Ireland, the men folk of Killorglin travel the twelve ten miles or so up into the Macgillycuddy's Reeks looking for the biggest 'he goat' they can find. The goats are brought back to the town, weighed, and measured, with the winner crowned King Puck (the goat that is, not his finder).

King Puck becomes the centre of attraction during three days of entertainment, partying, revelry, debauchery, and excitement. When the fair reaches a climax towards the end of the third day, the goat is dressed in a cloak with ribbons, loaded into a cart and paraded through the town as a hero.

It is said that this tradition dates to the 1600s when Cromwell and his army were pillaging the countryside at the foot of the Macgillycuddy Reeks. A herd of wild goats took flight before the raiders, and the he-goat or 'Puck' broke away on his own and lost contact with the herd. The goat eventually found its way to Killorglin and alerted the inhabitants of the approaching danger. The people then decided to host a festival in the goat's honour each year.

Leaving Killorglin, I make my way eastwards along the banks of the River Laune on the N72 towards Killarney where I catch my first glimpse of Carrantuohill, Ireland's highest mountain, eight miles away up to my right. Standing at 1,041 metres above sea level, I'm delighted to see it for the first time.

The name brings back memories of my old geography teacher Sammy Lyons. Even after almost forty years I can vividly recall Sammy calling me up in front of the class to a large map of Ireland, where he said. 'Point out the Macgillycuddy's Reeks to the class Lowry'.

My somewhat vague gesture towards south-west Ireland seemed to satisfy him and I sat down again with a sense of relief.

Passing the northern end of Lough Leane where Mahony's Point juts out into the Lough, I have just four miles left to cycle. Twenty minutes later and the 'Welcome to Killarney Town' road sign signals the end of a hard day in the saddle.

Cycling down into Killarney town centre, every second gaudily painted house, seems to have a B&B sign outside. 'Should have no problem finding a B&B here,' I mutter to myself.

Choosing the nearest B&B to the town centre called Lissmore House, I ring the bell. The lady of the house looks at me with what I can only call suspicion, I can only assume that she doesn't often get sweaty, lycra clad, heavily laden cyclists on her doorstep. Nevertheless, she offers me a room for the night, but I'm amazed to be asked to pay on arrival for the first time on the trip. Perhaps Killarney's visitors have a habit of doing an early morning runner without paying their bill, or maybe I just look the type who might do a runner without paying?

Killarney is one of Ireland's best-known towns and as its reputation as a tourist destination is legendary and I'm really looking forward to seeing it, as I've never been before.

The town centre is alive with tourists as I wander down the aptly named 'Main Street' looking for a quiet bar for my early evening pint. A quiet pint seems out of the question as, even though it is only late June, the bars are all packed with tourists. Loud Irish music blares out from huge speakers mounted on the walls outside.

Rows and rows of tacky souvenir shops, bars and restaurants line the narrow streets. Shop windows are crammed full of Irish souvenirs such as leprechauns, ashtrays, shillelaghs, and 'genuine' Irish key rings whilst a veritable procession of jaunting-cars jammed full of American tourists, smoking huge cigars and taking photographs, canter up and down.

Honor Tracy sums this up in the 1950s when she travelled round Ireland:

> *'Killarney was full of Americans in merrily coloured ties and attractive shoes. They were jogging through the streets in jaunting-cars, which they believed was the native method of travel. Killarney appears to bind them in a spell.'*

Street entertainers and musicians ply their trade every few yards, along with beggars, souvenir sellers and various dodgy looking characters. The drivers of jaunting cars sing Irish folk songs as they tout for business and the pubs all advertise traditional Irish food and musical entertainment.

Strolling along Main Street I pass at least half a dozen 'human statues.' You know – those people who paint their faces silver, black or any other colour, stand on a box and only move when you drop a few coins into their box. If you just stroll past, they have this knack of following you with their eyes as if to say 'you tight b…..d.' One of the other features of Killarney's Main Street is children standing on street corners holding tall poles with signs on the top advertising a restaurant, pub or a club. As you pass by, they hand you a small card tempting you in with an offer of a free pint or a discount on your meal.

My guidebook confirms that Killarney has been the Mecca for beggars and pickpockets for a couple of hundred years, so I keep my hands firmly on my wallet.

An anonymous visitor to Killarney in 1838 complained of:

> *'hundreds of men, women and children…all seemed bent on one determined purpose….that of robbing the unfortunate traveller.'*

Robert Carlyle on arriving in Killarney in 1849 just at the end of the great famine, wrote that:

> *'I found a chaos of hungry porters, inn agents, lodging agents and beggars storming around you like ravenous dogs round carrion.'*

I get the impression though, as I wander down main street, that the real Killarney might still be out there somewhere under this thin veneer brought about by mass tourism.

Strolling up College Street, I pass an impressive statue looking down rather disdainfully upon this whole tacky tourist scene. Out comes the guidebook, which reveals that this is the Sky-Woman of Kerry, a masterpiece of sculpture by Seamus Murphy. She stands proudly with the Macgillycuddy Reeks rising behind her like some majestic backdrop, her head wrapped in white satin in a classic Irish pose – hand over heart with harp in the other hand. At her feet are etched the names of many famous Irish poets: Geoffrey Donahue, Pierce Ferriter, Owen Roe O'Sullivan and Egan O'Rahilly.

As most of the bars and restaurants are packed, I opt for a carry out Pizza and head back to the Lissmore house – another day bites the dust.

Day's statistics: 39.4 miles – Average speed – 8.3mph – Time taken – 4hours 42 minutes – Max speed – 25mph

Chapter 17

Day 14 – Killarney to Kenmare (23 miles)

It's day fourteen and the sun is shining as I set off out of Killarney along the N71. I'm aware that today is going to be one of my hardest days cycling on the trip and I mentally prepare myself for it. I'm heading for Moll's gap through the mountains, where at 853 feet above sea level it will be the highest point on my trip.

The road is relatively flat as follows the eastern shore of Lough Leane, the largest of the three lakes in the area. As I cycle merrily along, I ponder on the reason why it's called a Lough whilst the other two are called lakes. The Loughs of Killarney somehow does not seem to have the same ring about it as the Lakes of Killarney, but never mind, this is Ireland after all.

Killarney's lakes have been steeped in tradition, folklore, and romanticism for many years. During the eighteenth century they were the place to be seen as tourists came in their thousands to see their beauty. Queen Victoria was a regular visitor and was so taken with Killarney's lakes that she had a large royal barge brought over from London so that she could take Albert and their children on regular trips on them.

With the early afternoon sun glistening off the calm waters of Lough Leane, I pass what can only be described as an Irish bus depot – a lay-by filled with a variety of horse drawn carts commonly known as jaunting cars. The jaunting car has been one of Ireland's traditional modes of transport for centuries and in Killarney they have certainly used this tradition as a 'nice little earner.' I'm told that the drivers can often be quite vigorous in their efforts to tempt you to part with your Punts for a short jaunt, a distance that you could walk in an hour or so, but the American tourists seem to get a huge kick out of a trip in an Irish Jaunting Car.

A couple of miles out of the town I pass the entrance to Muckross Abbey, one of Ireland's major ecclesiastical sites. Founded in 1448 as a Franciscan friary for the Observantine Franciscans by Donal MacCarthy Mor, the Abbey has a violent history. It has been damaged and reconstructed many times when the friars were often subjected to raids by marauding groups and persecuted by Cromwellian forces.

A mile or so further on and I pass the entrance to Muckross House, a house and grounds that were presented by William Bowers Bourn and Arthur Rose Vincent in 1932 to the Irish nation. It became the first National Park in the Republic of Ireland.

Looming over the house and gardens away up to my left, at a height of 1,755 feet, Torc Mountain casts its shadow over the lakes, whilst towering several miles behind, even higher at 2,788 feet, Mangerton Mountain with its extinct volcano, dominates the landscape.

High up near the summit of Mangerton lies the Punch Bowl, a lake over 820 feet deep with water even blacker than Guinness. According to legend, if a childless woman climbs the mountain and drinks from the lake, she will have a child - again one of those appealing legends for which Ireland is so famous.

Another legend about the Punch Bowl tells of two young men who went up for a swim one day in high summer. After swimming around for several minutes, one of the men noticed that the other was missing, and in a state of panic swam to the shore and ran down the mountain to get help. After dragging the lake for days, the local police were unable to find the body. Three weeks later the young man gets a letter from his friend saying, 'I've arrived quite safe in Australia can you send me my clothes.'

Just as the road starts to swing around the lake to the right, a tourist sign catches my eye – Torc Waterfall, so I pull into the small car park to have a look. Leaving my bike chained to a fence, I walk the quarter of a mile or so up the well-worn path to the waterfall in the company of a busload of noisy and excited American tourists. I've seen a few waterfalls in my time, but this one leaves me somewhat underwhelmed, but the Yanks certainly seemed to think it is quite something. According to the sign, the word Torc comes from the Irish translation of a 'wild boar', and the area is associated with legends involving wild boars.

Regretting wasting a half an hour or so admiring this 'magnificent' waterfall, I walk back to my steed, climb back into the saddle and head on along the N71. The road swings south-west at the end of the lake and the climb I have been dreading (looking forward to actually) begins. As I start to ascend, I can see the magical Macgillycuddy Reeks with Ireland's highest peak, Carrauntoohill at 3,415 feet above sea level, standing out against a clear blue sky.

The delightful hills of Kerry rise away on both sides of the road, whilst big fluffy clouds drift silently over the peaks, as it twists and turns ever upwards. The scenery is so mesmerising that the effort is temporarily forgotten. Lush fields now give way to harsh, uncultivated hillsides with huge rocks sticking out like giant bunions.

Passing the long narrow Upper Lake, I slog on ever upwards towards Moll's Gap. Every time my thumb flicks the lever up out of the lowest gear, my bike almost stops, but despite the temptation to get off and walk, I press on upwards at a miserly three miles an hour.

Even the sheep grazing on either side of the road give me glances as if to say 'silly bugger' as this sweaty idiot in lycra huffs and puffs his way ever upwards in the late morning sun.

As I fully expected, this ascent is not for the fainthearted, and whilst my legs are beginning to turn to jelly, the superb views are now lost on me as I rise out of the saddle and fix my eyes on the front wheel.

It's a relief to pause for a few minutes rest and a well-earned drink at a small gift shop and cafeteria nestling into the side of the mountain overlooking the Upper Lake. My guidebook informs me that this little layby is called 'ladies view'. This was a favourite spot of Queen Victoria in the early 1860s where, along with her ladies-in-waiting, she would frequently visit to pass away a few restful hours admiring the superb views across the valley.

This route up through the mountains of South Kerry has been a favourite haunt of cyclists for over 100 years and at Ladies View I have the opportunity to chat to several of my fellow cyclists as we enjoy some well-earned refreshment. Most of those I chat to are locals out for a day's cycling,

or visitors to the area who have hired bikes for the day. I must confess feeling just that little bit superior as their jaws drop, when I tell them that I'm cycling 1,000 miles around the whole of Ireland and have been in the saddle for fourteen days.

With words of encouragement and praise ringing in my ears, I set off again up the N71 for the final push to the summit (sounds like an Everest expedition). After another hour of torture in low gear watching my knees rise and fall every two seconds, I pass Looscaunagh Lough and for ever upwards towards Molls Gap. Stopping once again at a car park just before the Gap where the N71 and R568 meet, I get even better views of the mountains and lakes with the Macgillycuddy Reeks rising away in majestic splendour to the north-west. Carrantuohill stands out impressively over the whole panorama. Back over my shoulder to the north-east, I can make out Mangerton Mountain again and directly north Purple Mountain, Tomes Mountain, and the Gap of Dunloe. From this point, I get some of the most stunning views I have ever seen and unlikely to be bettered anywhere in the world. You are simply surrounded by a whole series of beautiful hills and mountains. The harshness of the mountain's dissolves away into the softness of rich and fertile valleys to the north, south, east, and west – truly stunning scenery and well worth the effort.

With Moll's Gap in sight at last, I struggle on upwards through a short tunnel before eventually reaching the summit. Without doubt this is the most demanding section of the trip so far, but also the most rewarding, as the sense of achievement and satisfaction is immense.

One of the earliest books on cycling in Ireland, *Bicycling 1874 – A Textbook for Early Riders* gave Moll's Gap a five-star rating, but it fails to mention the torture imposed upon the rider to get there.

The gap is named after Moll Kissane who ran a shebeen, a small pub, on a rocky breach during the construction of the original Kenmare to Killarney Road in the 1820s. She became popular for selling home brewed poitin, whiskey, to the hardy men who worked on the road.

Stopping just before reaching the gap, my first impression is that a giant has ripped a chunk out of the mountain and just tossed it away. Looking around, there is no sign of a huge chunk of rock anywhere in the vicinity, perhaps he lobbed it back into Looscaunagh Lough?

During the eighteenth century, this journey through the mountains between County Kerry and County Cork was a daunting expedition for travellers. Writing about the crossing in 1780, Arthur Young in his book A Tour in Ireland, recounts that:

> *'me and my fellow travellers felt agitation and suspense at the various horrid grotesque and unusual forms in which the mountains rise and the rocks bulge.'*

Young said that his chaise had to be moved over the rocks with levers and ropes by six stout lads provided by the local landlord.

During the 1840s, Alexander Nimmo (that man again) was contracted to build a new road through the mountains linking the two counties. His road changed a hazardous mountainous adventure into a modern-day tourist route.

With a last wave to Killarney, I leave the shadow of the gap and cycle on down the N71 towards Kenmare. On this side of the mountain another beautiful vista opens before me. Kenmare Bay and the southern section of the Ring of Kerry looks like a rich tapestry in the hazy afternoon sunshine away down below in the distance.

After the rigours of the previous climb, I career down the side of one of the most beautiful mountains in Ireland at forty miles an hour. There is a special feeling about descending at such a speed, just on the edge of control and common sense. Ernest Hemingway once wrote:

> *'It is by riding a bicycle that you learn the contours of a country best, since you have to sweat up the hills and coast down them.'*

He was certainly correct.

Setting off from Killarney earlier this morning, my target for the day was Bantry town, but with thirty-five miles still to cycle, and with the effort in climbing up to Moll's Gap taking its toll, Kenmare seems a more realistic target for my overnight stop. Descending at a rapid rate of knots down into Kenmare, not for the first time on the trip, the weather once again begins to change. The sunshine of the past few hours has now turned into a light rain – a heavy mist in Ireland, but this heavy mist is now making me very wet and uncomfortable as it sweeps into my face from the Atlantic.

Half an hour later and I'm crossing over the Finnahy River and into Kenmare town centre. The town centre seems devoid of B&Bs, so I find myself on the Cork Road out of the town where a series of large houses border a golf course. Cycling up the gravel path of the Mylestone House, the first house I come to with a B&B vacancies sign hanging outside, I knock on the door. At the end of another hard day in saddle, I readily accept a room from the hosts Fiona and John Sullivan.

After a nice hot shower and a twenty-minute nap, I stroll from the Mylestone down into the centre of Kenmare for a pint of the black stuff and some food. By now the earlier rain has gone and it's a beautiful evening as I settle down with my pint at a table outside Mulcahys on the main street. After such a hard day, I'm enjoying my cold pint and contentedly watching the world go by, when a gentleman plonks himself beside me. Despite the fact that there are several other empty tables nearby, he chooses mine. As you well know by now, in Ireland people are very sociable so I nod to him and raise my glass in acknowledgment.

Not the best dressed man about town, he produces a battered old can of Guinness from a plastic bag and begins to slurp the contents in a series of gulps, all the while giving me the thumbs up. I quickly realise that I might just have bumped into the town alcoholic and for the next ten minutes or so he entertains me with his life story, at least I think that's what he is telling me as the words tumble so quickly out of his mouth in his thick Kerry accent. Eventually one of the bar staff comes out and quickly moves him on.

'Sorry about that sur,' he says, 'he's harmless enough but he does annoy the visitors.'

As it's has been almost a week since I gorged on a fish and chip supper in Donegal, and as most of the restaurants in Kenmare seem to be full, I indulge myself to another of those high cholesterol, high fat meals. All is well with the world as I walk along on a nice summer evening in Kenmare, munching fish and chips from a bag after a couple of pints of Guinness – bliss.

Day's statistics: 22.8 miles – Average speed – 9.5mph – Time taken – 2hours 24 minutes – Max speed – 29mph

Note: Sadly, four years after I made my trip, John Sullivan passed away and Fiona sold the B & B.

Chapter 18

Day 15 – Kenmare to Skibereen (52 miles)

After a superb full Irish breakfast in the Mylestone, I bid Fiona and John goodbye and set off out of Kenmare on day fifteen. The first few miles on the N71 are reasonably flat and make for easy cycling, but on reaching the village of Bonane, the road begins to rise steadily, and I have to drop down through the gears as the Caha mountains sweep up steeply on both sides - I know that I am in for another day of hard climbing.

Stopping for a drink in a layby, I'm treated to the sight of a farmer and his dog having a problem getting his sheep into a pen. The sheep are playing cat and mouse with the dog. Just as it has them nicely corralled ready to enter the pen, one of them makes a race for it away from the group and when the dog then gallops off after the single rogue sheep, the rest scatter and the whole process starts again.

Feeling rather sorry for the dog, I say to the farmer, 'Looks as though you're having a bit of a problem with that lot.'

'Sure you're not helping, keep quiet and don't distract them,' he snaps back.

Suitably admonished and feeling rather sheepish (excuse the pun), I watch as the drama unfolds for another twenty minutes or so before the sheep are eventually persuaded to enter the pen. I feel like clapping in appreciation, but decide that as it wouldn't be very tactful, I remount and head on my merry way.

An hour or so later, when I reach the highest point in this part of south Kerry, I enter my fifteenth county in eighteen days – Cork, the largest county in Ireland.

On the border of the two counties, three huge man-made tunnels slice through the mountains. When I emerge from the final tunnel at the top of the pass, the view directly in front of me is quite stupendous. G.B. Shaw called this *'Ireland's Riviera'* and I have to agree with his sentiments that:

> *'The views across Bantry Bay are the finest view in all the countries of the earth.'*

The long snaking descent down the N 71 into Glengarriff is a cyclist's bliss as I freewheel for around four miles, whilst admiring the views away down towards Bantry Bay.

When the road eventually levels out, I cycle over the river Glengarriff, past the Woods Nature Reserve and into the small town of Glengarriff. Sheltered on three sides by high tree-lined hills, Glengarriff looks out along the Beara peninsula towards the Atlantic Ocean. During the second half of the nineteenth century, it was a very popular holiday retreat for wealthy Victorians who would take the train from Dublin to Bantry and then a paddle steamer across the Bay to Glengarriff. When William M.Thackeray visited the town in 1842 and he was certainly right when he wrote: *'of the astonishing beauty of Glengarriff'.*

Pressing on along the N71, I cross the Coomhola River and along the shore of the bay past the harbour and on south-east towards Bantry town. Bantry Bay, a twenty-five-mile-long expanse of sheltered water, was a major strategic anchorage for the British Navy during the 17th and 18th centuries. At that time, it was little more than a basic anchorage with a modest shore establishment, all protected by some useful if unimposing fortifications.

The base was modernised and strengthened at the end of the nineteenth century, as was the fleet, in response to the rising power of the French—and more particularly the German—navy. It was deemed the 'Irish Gibraltar' in 1902 and 'the key of the Atlantic'. During World War I it was an important strategic base for the British Navy.

As I cycle along the shoreline, I get my first glimpse of Whiddy Island, a four-square mile scrap land that is now home to a mere twenty people. During the latter part of World War I, it was the location of a U.S. Naval Air Station used for Anti-Submarine Warfare patrols by Curtiss H-16 seaplanes.

A large oil terminal was constructed on the island in the late 1960s by Gulf Oil. Designed to accommodate the largest super-tankers sailing directly from the Middle East, tragedy struck in January 1979 when a French tanker, the Betelgeuse, was unloading a cargo of crude oil at the terminal. The tanker exploded killing fifty people. The terminal was never fully repaired and in 1986 it was transferred to the Irish government to hold the Irish strategic oil reserve.

A few minutes later and I'm cycling into Bantry, a town of around 3,000 residents. I stop for a short rest and a drink at Wolfe Tone Square in the town centre, a square that commemorates Theobald Wolfe Tone, a leader during the 1798 rebellion.

I spot a Statue of St Brendan the Navigator in the square, a gift from Gulf Oil when the company first set up camp in Bantry in the 1960s it says.

Leaving Bantry, I cycle on south-west along the N71 on the south side of the bay. It's a beautiful day, and as the bay is calm, I decide to take the opportunity to sample the wonderful warm waters fed by the Gulf Stream. Approaching a small jetty, I notice some people frolicking in the water. Propping the bike against a low wall adjacent to the jetty, I take my clothes, still damp from the previous days rain, out of my panniers and spread them out along the top of the wall to dry in sun.

For the first time on the trip, I don my swimming trunks and prepare to join the locals for a dip. I've worked up a real sweat cycling over the mountains, and the thought of relaxing in the warm water of the Gulf Stream after a hard day's cycle is mouth-watering. I'm told that the Gulf Stream which comes up from the Gulf of Mexico washes the shores of Kerry with warm waters and that some people here swim in the sea all year round as the temperature varies little.

Stepping boldly into the inviting calm blue water, it takes my breath away – yes, it's freezing – and I mean freezing, it's so cold I can't feel my toes before I even get up to my knees. I have swum in some pretty cold waters in the past, but this is something else.

'Come on in,' shouts one of the locals happily frolicking in the water – 'it's lovely'.

I smile and wave, but my instinct is turn on my heels and head back up the slipway. This hardened long-distance cyclist with leg muscles like iron bars is baulking at the thought of swimming in Bantry Bay in late June.

Not wishing to be seen as a bit of a softie, I wade on down until the water is up to my waist and just dive in. When the shock of the icy cold-water hits me I gasp for air.

After nonchalantly swimming a couple of yards, I wave again and make a beeline for the jetty. 'Not got much time' I lie. If anyone tells you that the waters of Bantry Bay in late June are warm, don't believe them. Fortunately, the sun is still blazing from an azure blue sky and sitting on the sea wall, I quickly warm up whilst my clothes dry in its warm rays.

After a refreshing drink and an energy bar, I repack my panniers and set off again due directly south on the N71 towards Skibbereen.

The road begins to twist, turn, rise, and fall like a roller coaster as I cycle on through the villages of Scart (thought that was a computer lead) and Letterlickey, past Barnaghgeehy forest and on towards Ballydehob.

Stopping for a rest at Ballydehob, I consult my guidebook again. A small town with a few hundred souls, Ballydehob is situated on an estuary off Roaring Water Bay, one of the most southerly of the five great inlets in south-west Ireland. The Bay is dotted with a multitude of small emerald-green grassy islands like green gemstones nestling on a blue carpet.

Three survivors of the Titanic disaster came from the town. All three bought tickets for the ill-fated journey from Barry's Shipping Agency in the town.

As I progress on this trip of a lifetime, my education about Ireland and its people expands by the hour. Ballydehob's most famous resident was one Danno O'Mahony. As someone who has been interested in sport all my life, I was astonished to discover that in 1933, while serving in the Irish Army, O'Mahony distinguished himself as an athlete. He set military records for the hammer throw and the 56lb weight throw, records that were not broken until the 1990s. Also, an accomplished boxer and wrestler, he was brought to America in 1934 by a Boston wrestling promoter, Paul Bowser. The following year, aged 22, having only begun wrestling two years previously

Danno became the undisputed wrestling champion of the world, resulting in much celebrating back in Ballydehob. I guess a few pints of the black stuff were consumed.

Leaving Danno's birthplace and with only 12 miles more to cycle until reaching Skibereen, my target for tonight, I press on through Aghadown and along the north shone of the Ilen estuary.

Passing the Abbeystrewry cemetery I stop for a few minutes to pay tribute to the 8,000-10,000 unidentified souls who were laid to rest here during what was probably the most tragic period in Irish history. During the Irish potato famine years of the mid-1800s, Skibbereen was considered the epicentre of one of the most appalling human disasters in nineteenth century Europe. Between 1845 and 1849, at least a million people died of fever and malnutrition in Ireland.

Those who lost their lives are remembered today in the Famine Heritage Centre where an audio-visual display re-enacts a variety of scenes from that terrible time. Although I do not have time to visit the centre, my guidebook tells me of a poignant quote from a Major Parker in 1846, a quote that to me sums up the awful reality of the situation:

> *A woman with a dead child in her arms was begging in the streets yesterday. The guard of the mill told me he saw a man and three dead children lying in the roadside a few miles from this place. Nothing can exceed the miserable state of this place.*

In 1791 the population of Ireland was 8.5 million, but by 1850 at least one million people had died of fever and malnutrition, often in the most horrific conditions, whilst another million emigrated to get away from the disaster.

More than 50% of the children in Skibbereen were admitted to the workhouse in 1846 where they died a slow and painful death of hunger, whilst many more died of a fever epidemic. Those unfortunate families are remembered today in its Famine Heritage Centre.

When I reach Skibbereen town centre, I discover that B&Bs seem to be a bit thin on the ground. Once again, I'm forced to expend some extra energy exploring the roads in the outskirts of the town. Glancing down a small side

road, I notice a large crowd shouting, cheering and waving their arms. Curiosity gets the better of me, and despite the physical discomfort of a long day in the saddle, I cycle down the side road towards the group. A sign by the side of the road informs me that 'Road Bowling is in Progress'. I've just stumbled upon a real live Road Bowling competition.

As I'm to discover later, Road Bowling (also called long bullets) is a very popular sport in County Cork, and it makes my day to be able to witness it for the first time. The exact origins of the sport of Road Bowling are somewhat vague, but one theory is that it may have originated in Holland around the end of the sixteenth century and been introduced to Ireland when William of Orange invaded in 1690. It is documented that his soldiers played the game on their days off from fighting using the severed heads of the English settlers from the previous day's battle. Another theory is that Irish patriots robbed English cannonballs and rolled them down a country lane by the light of a full moon – take your pick. It's not made it as an Olympic sport yet, but perhaps one day when the Olympics come to Dublin.

Picture the scene in front of my eyes – a narrow country road on the outskirts of Skibbereen, County Cork late on a summer afternoon. A couple of hundred people, mainly men in their late to middle agė are whooping and hollering. Their 'man' sprints down the middle of the road and unleashes a solid metal ball the size of a small shot. The road is not closed to traffic and a few motorists are kept patiently waiting until the projectile is on its way bouncing and crashing down the middle of the road. The 'boss man', or at least the portly red-faced gentleman who seems to be in charge, then waves the cars through as the crowd parts. Once any waiting cars have passed, the crowd make their way after the two competitors to the spot where the bowl/shot has come to rest.

'What's the game all about?' I enquire of one of the locals at the rear of the group.

'Oh, sure it's a grand sport now. The two boyos hurl (to throw or fling with great force or vigor) that there ball down a three-mile stretch of this road, whichever one completes the course in the lesser number of hurls, wins – a bit like golf, it's as simple as that. I've got 500 Punts on yer man there to win,' he points.

The excitement generated by the crowd is astonishing; One man tells me that huge sums of money will change hands at the end of this Sunday afternoon stroll down a country road in West Cork.

Following the bowlers and their supporters down the road, I come across a group of people ferreting around in the dense hedgerow by the side of the road like golfers looking for a ball in the rough. The agitation in their faces and actions are intense as they stamp around in the waist high grass with a sense of urgency.

'What's happened?' I ask a bystander.

'Sure the ball's lost', he says in a matter-of-fact tone of voice.

'So what happens if they can't find it?' I add.

'Sure no problem, he will take his next throw from where it was last seen darting into the verge as it hit a bump in the road.'

Just then a shout goes up, they have found it, a line is chalked across the road and 'yer man' prepares for his next hurl.

This rare sport is so engaging that at one point I'm not paying attention to my balance and forgetting to de-cleat, I fall off the bike to my intense embarrassment and the amusement of the spectators.

Exhausted after a hard day in the saddle and after bidding the bowlers farewell, I head off in search of a B&B.

The N71 (I seem to have been on the N71 for days) out of the town towards Leap looks promising and I eventually find a nice house just a ten-minute walk from the centre of the town. After settling in, set off looking for my usual nourishment. Skibbereen is (sorry was) the temperance centre of Ireland during the latter part of the nineteenth and the early part of the twentieth century, a fact confirmed by a plaque on the wall of a building as I stroll past: 'First Temperance Hall 1833 – 1964', it proudly proclaims. I find it hard to believe that anywhere in Ireland could have been the least bit temperate.

*Although I did not have time to visit it on my trip, a year or so later my wife and I did visit and were quite moved by what we saw and heard. An audio-visual display re-enacts a variety of scenes from that awful time and a poignant quote from a Major Parker in 1846, to me summed up the awful reality of the situation: 'A woman with a dead child in her arms was begging in the streets yesterday. The guard of the mill told me he saw a man and three dead children lying in the roadside a few miles from this place. Nothing can exceed the miserable state of this place.'

Whilst the blight on the potato crop caused the problem in the first instance, the main burden of the blame for the awful tragedy seems to lie with the English landlords, who failed to feed the starving population. Barley, wheat and vegetables all continued to thrive in the rich green meadows, but the landlords exported them to a lucrative English market for their own financial gain. The value of wheat doubled almost overnight and to this day this abject failure to feed the Irish people is often likened to the treatment of the Jews in the early 1940's in Germany. However, I will leave you to make up your own views on this most sensitive subject, but the famine exhibition in the Skibbereen Heritage Centre paints a most disturbing picture of the fate of many people from this part of Ireland in the mid 1800's and is well worth a visit if you happen to be in the area.

Day's statistics: 52.4 miles – Average speed – 9.3mph – Time taken – 5hours 36 minutes – Max speed – 27.00mph

Chapter 19

Day 16 – Skibereen to Kinsale (47 miles)

It's day sixteen and with two thirds of my trip complete, I leave Skibbereen and head east towards Kinsale in high spirits. The sun is shining out of an azure blue sky and I'm singing to myself as I leisurely turn over the pedals.

At the village of Leap, I leave the busy N71 and follow the R597 along the shore of Glandore estuary into the small village of the same name. A picturesque, quaint little harbour village, Glandore nestles snugly at the foot of high wooded hillsides that rise steeply on two sides. The village is so beautiful that I just have to stop for a drink and recharge my batteries by the sheltered harbour. Sitting on the harbour wall I watch the small boats coming and going and the children playing on the shingle with the blue Atlantic just beyond – idyllic.

A cluster of huge houses, nay mansions, dot the hillsides overlooking the bay. It's anyone's guess as to how much one of these pads would cost. One of the most impressive of these 'palaces' is the holiday residence of Tony O'Reilly, a former buccaneering Irish rugby winger in the 1960s and now a successful businessman.

Reluctantly leaving the peace and tranquillity of Glandore, I cycle on inland over the River Roury and into Rosscarbery. A small village situated at the head of an estuary of the same name, Rosscarbery has seven pubs and a church clustered around its quadrangular square, with multi-coloured houses standing cheek by jowl between the pubs and the church. The village was home to the School of Ross, a major centre of learning, and at one time it was a university town.

The people of Rosscarbery came in for some stick from Susan and Thomas Cahill in their entertaining book *'A Literary Guide to Ireland'* published in 1973 when the Cahills rather cruelly wrote:

You cannot be more than an hour or so in these parts without running smack into the gleeful, hopeless inefficiency of Carberry people.

A bit harsh to say the least, but I'm sure that they are just as friendly and charming as the rest of the West Cork people.

Leaving Rosscarbery, I cycle on over the five-hundred-yard bridge that spans the shallow estuary that opens onto Rosscarbery bay. The sweeping beach of the bay stretches to my right and away in the distance I can see the outline of Galley Head lighthouse, clearly visible in the morning sunshine.

Continuing inland towards Clonakilty, I spot a signpost pointing to the left and tilting at 45 degrees: 'Michael Collins' Birthplace – 2 miles' it proclaims. Collins, an Irish revolutionary, soldier, politician, and a leading figure in the early twentieth century Irish struggle for independence was born in the townland Woodfield, Coolcraheen just up to my left. Chairman of the Provisional Government of the Irish Free State from January 1922 until his assassination in August 1922, Collins gained fame as a guerrilla warfare strategist during the struggle. He planned and directed many successful attacks on British forces, such as the 'Bloody Sunday' assassinations of key British intelligence agents in November 1920.

As the day is now 'wearing on' as they say in these parts, I resist the temptation to visit Collins' birthplace and head on towards Kinsale, my target for the day.

Soon I arrive at Clonakilty. A good-sized market town of around 3,000 inhabitants, Clonakilty was founded by Richard Boyle the Earl of Cork in 1598, when he planted it with a hundred English families. It was a Protestant town from which Catholics were excluded, but today Clonakility is now very Irish and very Catholic – the original Presbyterian chapel is now the Post Office.

Four miles inland from Clonakilty lies the small village of Ballinascarty. This small village was the birthplace of William Ford, father of Henry Ford, the founder of the Ford Motor Company. At the height of the famine in 1847 William Ford packed up the family belongings and walked from Ballinascarty to Cobh, a distance of around thirty miles, from where they emigrated to America. After settling in Dearborn Michigan, William's wife gave birth to Henry in 1863. When Henry began his expansion of the Ford Motor Company in 1917, he opened the first production plant outside America in Cork.

It's a beautiful day and I'm making good progress when I leave the N71 again just outside Clonakilty and join the R600 towards Kinsale. Tucking my head down over the handlebars, I soon reach Timoleague, a small village situated at the head of the Arigideen estuary. Timoleague and much of the adjacent country belonged to the Hodnetts, an English family who settled in the area from Shropshire. During the reign of Henry III, a great battle was fought at near the village between the Hodnetts, under Lord Phillip Hodnett, and the Barrys, under Lord Barrymore. The Hodnetts were routed, and their leader was killed with the Barrymores became the owners of Timoleague until the 1800s, when it was purchased by the Travers family.

Built in 1320 by the Franciscan monks, the ruins of a Franciscan friary stand on a hillside overlooking the town like a silent, ghostly sentinel.

Crossing the Arigideen river, I cycle on along the R600 as it hugs the shoreline of the picturesque Arigideen estuary. Over on the far shore, I can just make out a series of multi-coloured holiday homes, that from this distance look like those little hundred and thousands I used to sprinkle on top of my ice cream cone as a child.

Soon the road turns inland again and drops gently down into Ballinspittle. Just outside this small village with a population of 220, I stumble upon its claim to fame - a statue of the Virgin Mary standing in a grotto by the side of the R600. I'm curious as to why this modest statue of one of Ireland's most famous saints could be of any great significance to a small village in County Cork and why many thousands of pilgrim's flock to the village each year. As I'm due a drink and snack break, I stop to read the plaque below the statue.

It's fame and attraction soon become obvious when I discover that apparently several local people have seen this two-metre-high concrete statue actually move. The plaque reads:

'The Lourdes Grotto of our Lady and St Bernadette was erected by the people of Ballinspittle and blessed on the feast of the Immaculate Conception December the 8th 1954.'

Sitting on a bench on the opposite side of the road I stare at it intently, not daring to take my eyes off it for a second, waiting for the miracle to happen. Are my eyes playing tricks on me or did that statue really move? The hairs on the back of my neck are standing on end, similar to my experience back in Knock. Glancing up at her face I'm sure I detected a grin around the corners of her mouth.

After sitting looking at the statue for about twenty minutes I give up, wave the Virgin Mary goodbye, and set off up the hill towards Kinsale. I can't resist one last glance over my shoulder at the statue as I pedal away. I'm convinced that she will move as soon as I turn my back, but other than spending the night in a layby outside Ballinspittle, I'm not going to find out if the phenomenon actually does happen.

With six miles left to cycle, I press on along the N600. Cycling along the south side of the river Bandon, the road descends steeply down to the

Archdeacon Duggan bridge that spans the river. The bridge was named after Father Tom Duggan. Father Duggan served in the British army in the first World War and ended up as a prisoner of war. When the 2nd world war broke out, he volunteered again for the British army was awarded an OBE by King George VI.

With just a mile or so left to cycle, I pass the Viking Wharf and into the town. Weaving my way through the heavy afternoon traffic into the town centre, I keep my eyes peeled for a B&B. It would seem however, that every B&B in Kinsale has a 'no vacancy' sign hanging outside. Rather than expend more energy cycling around, I decide to visit the tourist office.

'Kinsale is very busy this time of year, but we'll hive a luke for ye.' the lovely assistant tells me.

I begin to get a little more concerned when she draws a blank with her first five phone calls. The thought of another eighteen miles cycling to Cork doesn't appeal to me, but fortunately, the sixth call comes up trumps.

'Murphy's Farmhouse have a room available, but it is about mile out of town high up on a hillside overlooking the harbour.' She says with a smile. Gratefully accepting the offer, I set off for Murphy's Farmhouse following the directions the assistant has given me.

They take me along the side of the river Bandon and up a steep hill on the Lower Road. Reaching the top, I look around me for a B&B sign but there is no sign of one, all I see in front of me is a farmyard and I'm beginning to wonder if the directions I have been given at the tourist office are correct.

This just looks like your average working farm, but when I knock on the door, I'm relieved when Mrs Murphy confirms that I am indeed at the right place and that she has a room available. She greets me with a welcoming smile and directs me to a barn at the rear of the house where I can leave my bike overnight.

Unpacking my panniers in the room I pick up what can only be described as a bit of a 'pong', but as I'm in a farm after all, I think nothing of it. When I head for the bathroom (no ensuite here), the slight pong turns into a real smell of what I am sure is from blocked drains. What's the odd whiff when you are knackered after a day in saddle anyway, so I just ignore it and lie down for my usual quick nap.

After dozing for an hour or so I set off to walk the mile or so back down the Lower Road into the town centre.

The town of Kinsale was founded by the Anglo-Normans in the twelfth century, and already a booming port, it received its first charter by King Edward III in 1334.

A mere fifteen miles from Cork, it was an excellent first stop for trading ships sailing from America and Europe, usually loaded with wine and salt. Today Kinsale's prosperity comes mainly from tourism, particularly popular with anglers and yachtsmen. Perhaps that's the reason why I had trouble finding accommodation for the night?

One of the most important battles in Irish history took place just outside Kinsale in 1601 when a pair of Ulster leaders, Hugh O'Neil, and his son in law Red Hugh O'Donnell attacked the English forces. The pair enlisted the help of the Spanish, who had been concerned about England's growing power in Europe and saw links with the Irish rebels as a way of attacking England through the back door as it were.

The Spanish landed some 3,500 men in the Brandon Estuary, quickly taking over the two castles that overlooked the harbour entrance. An English force of 12,000 men quickly surrounded the Spaniards and waited for the arrival of O'Neil and O'Donnell from the north. When they eventually arrived, their men were massacred by the English whilst the Spaniards sat in their castles and watched.

With the rebellion quashed, Kinsale became a predominantly English Protestant town and for the rest of the seventeenth century no Irishman or Catholic was permitted to live within its walls. The English influence that can still be seen today in the grand Georgian houses that line its streets.

After wandering around the narrow streets for half an hour admiring the large yachts moored in the harbour, I enjoy a couple of pints of the black stuff in two in several of the attractive pubs around the harbour side, followed by an excellent bar meal in the White House Hotel. Despite it still being early evening, the day's cycling has taken its toll and I slump into the back of a local taxi for the short journey up the hill to Murphy's.

Day's statistics: 47.00 miles – Average speed – 9.3mph – Time taken – 5hours 02 minutes – Max speed – 33.1mph

Chapter 20

Day 17 – Kinsale to Midleton (41 miles)

After another sumptuous full Irish breakfast (one that will shortly come back to haunt me), I load up my panniers and set off on the morning of day seventeen towards Ireland's second city, Cork. Before you Belfast folk take offence, I mean the second city in the Republic of Ireland, not the whole of the island.

It's raining that light soft Irish rain as I cycle along a fabulous stretch of the R600 for the first couple of miles out of Kinsale with my tyres hardly making a sound on the freshly laid tarmac. After crossing the river Stick, the luxury of this excellent flat surface soon reverts to the normal standard of Irish road, as it begins to twist and turn its way up an ever-increasing ascent through the villages of Belgooly and Riverstick.

After only about eight miles out of Kinsale, and unusual for so early in the day, I'm beginning to feel just a bit tired and slightly nauseous, but nonetheless I put my head down over the bars and press on as it begins to rain. With the rain now pouring down in torrents, the next couple of hours are hell in the saddle as each turn of the pedals becomes a huge effort. The rain is finding its way under my waterproofs through a multitude of channels. My glasses are steaming up as the rain drips off my nose.

The sound of aero engines indicates that I am nearing Cork airport and fortunately the heavy rain that has soaked me since just after Kinsale, seems to abate somewhat, as if to say, 'welcome to Cork, it's not always raining.'

By now I'm beginning to feel decidedly unwell. My muscles are aching, and I feel as though I might throw up at any time. I'm delighted to discover that this section of road towards Cork is now downhill with a very good cycle/bus lane, keeping me away from the traffic that whizzes past just yards away.

Approaching the busy Blackash roundabout on the outskirts of the city, I spot a sign – 'Ring Road East and Tunnel.' Stopping briefly to take a quick look at my map, it confirms that there is indeed a tunnel under the river Lee, good news indeed as I will be able to avoid the city centre and be well on my way east along the N25. Unfortunately, a large sign informs me that pedestrians and cyclists are banned from using the tunnel. Letting loose a torrent of expletives I contemplate breaking the law and making a run for it through the tunnel, but a vision of a headline in the Cork Independent brings me to my senses. 'Round Ireland cyclist jailed in Cork,' so I head towards the city centre.

The next two miles down into Cork along the N27 are scary to say the least. Having been in the saddle for eighteen days however, I'm now somewhat blasé about the dangers posed by mad Irish drivers. (I mean 'mad' in the sense of their carefree attitude towards the handling of their vehicles, not the fact that all Irish drivers are mad, if you know what I mean.)

The Cork drivers really do pose a threat today as I carefully negotiate my way around the city's one-way system, over the De Valera and Michael Michael Collins bridges and onto the N8 east.

Cork, with a population of around 180,000, is one of those cities that has a warm friendly feel to it – even on a damp and miserable July day. The old expression 'water, water everywhere' is particularly apt as the city sits on an island between two channels of the river Lee. To the east of the city, the river opens into Lough Mahon as it wends its way around to Cobh encircling Great Island to form the largest natural harbour in Europe.

Originally founded as a Viking settlement built on reclaimed marshland, Cork gets its name from the Irish word meaning marsh, although some people reckon it got its name because the city floats like a cork on waters of the Lee.

Whilst the city started life quietly enough in 600AD when St Finbar built a monastery overlooking the river, it slowly began to grow after a group of Norsemen invaded in 1000AD. The settlement enjoyed a period of stability for the next 300 years until Henry II arrived in the thirteenth century at a time when anti-English feelings were running high.

In 1921 Cork was the epicentre of the republican revolt against the British crown, the only city in Ireland dominated by the republicans who opposed the Anglo-Irish treaty signed in that year. This domination was short lived when it was soon taken by the Free State Army under the control of Michael Collins when he landed his troops at Passage West, near Cobh.

A few miles to the East of Cork lies the port of Cobh (pronounced Cove), probably one of the most famous ports in Irish history. Up until the middle of the twentieth century it was Ireland's main port for transatlantic passenger traffic, and it was from here that many Irish men and women left the mother country in droves over the centuries. During the first quarter of the twentieth century more than three quarters of a million young Irishmen and women left from Cobh for new lives all over the world, summed up so beautifully and sadly by Mr and Mrs S.C. Hall when they wrote about this sad exodus in their book simply called *Ireland*:

> We stood in the month of June on the quay at Cork to see some emigrants embark in one of the steamers for Falmouth, on the way to Australia. The band of exiles amounted to two hundred, and an immense crowd had gathered to bid them a long and last adieu. The scene was touching to a degree: it was impossible to witness it without heart-pain and tears. Mothers hung upon the necks of their athletic sons: young girls clung to their elder sisters: fathers-old white-headed men fell on their knees, with arms uplifted to heaven, imploring the protecting care of the Almighty on their departing children.

Cobh was also the last port of call for the ill-fated Titanic, picking up many Irish people before sailing to disaster out in the Atlantic and into the annals as probably the world's worst maritime disaster.

Crossing the River Glashaboy, I'm soon cycling east along the N25 on one of the worst roads of the entire trip. Potholes the size of small bomb craters abound, verges are littered with rocks, cans, broken glass and other sundry discarded items and it is a real challenge to keep the bike on an even keel. At least the authorities seem to be making some effort to improve the road as every few miles, road works with temporary traffic lights are in operation.

Following the northern banks of the River Lee eastward, I can just make out the exit from the northern end of the tunnel. Swearing again under my breath I bemoan the extra hour of hard cycling it has taken me to get to this point rather than the ten minutes it would have taken me to cycle through the tunnel but hey ho, that's life on a round Ireland cycle.

Cork dissolves into the distance behind me, and when the road surface improves considerably, I fairly whizz along on a nice flat section.

I seem to be the only non-mechanised vehicle on the road as cars and lorries zip past my right shoulder at high speed. As most seasoned cyclists will tell you, the biggest threat of an accident occurs when a huge juggernaut passes you at high speed when the vacuum created tends to suck you back into the middle of the road.

I'm so bored cycling along this flat section that I begin counting the dead animals littering the verges: a couple of rabbits, a cat, a squirrel, a hedgehog, and somebody's pet dog, have all met their maker on this stretch of road.

Cycling on along the shore of Slatty Water, past Fota Island and through Cobh Cross, I begin to feel even queasier. My energy levels are low despite downing vast quantities of energy drink.

The sun is beginning to break through the clouds as I near the town of Midleton, a town that is the home to the Old Midleton Distillery. The Distillery was set up by the Murphy brothers in 1820 and contains the world's largest pot still – a copper vessel with a capacity of 140,000 litres. The distillery produces several Irish whiskeys, including Jamesons, Redbreast and Paddy.

My target for the day is Youghall, nineteen miles further, but with my stomach just about in a state off utter revolt I decide to call it a day.

Under normal circumstances I would be looking forward a drop of the famous Jamesons, but I'm now feeling so bad that any thought of whiskey makes me feel even more queasy. Cycling up the main street looking for accommodation - B&B signs are not exactly jumping out at me – perhaps Midleton isn't too keen on visitors despite its world-famous distillery. With no sign of a tourist information office, the filling station seems like a good option and the young lad behind the counter just shakes his head when I enquire about a B&B, 'don't think there are any,' he says.

Climbing reluctantly back into the saddle, I cycle back up the main street for the second time and spot a well-worn B&B sign above a weather-beaten door. With no other choice, I knock on the door – no bell just one of those big brass knockers so popular in Ireland.

An elderly lady opens the door and eyes me up and down with what I can only describe as suspicion. After giving her my well-practised spiel about the trip she seems somewhat reluctant at first to offer me a room, but she relents, and waves me into a dark dismal passageway where she says I can leave my bike for the night.

By now I'm feeling really ill and in no mood to even consider looking elsewhere, so I gladly accept the small dark room overlooking the main street.

Collapsing on the bed completely exhausted, I lie for half an hour or so with a dreadful nauseous feeling coming and going. Although I don't feel like it, I make the effort to take a shower in the communal bathroom before forcing myself to get dressed and venture out into the town for some food.

Stepping out onto the pavement, that heavy nauseous feeling that has accompanied me all day begins to get even worse and for the first time on this trip I just don't fancy a pint of Guinness nor any food. I decide to give dinner a miss and head back for an early night.

Despite the feeling of nausea and cramps in my stomach, sleep comes quickly as I am exhausted, but after what seems like a matter of minutes, I'm sitting up in bed trying to keep the contents of my stomach in their rightful place. The battle is lost, and I just make it to the adjoining bathroom in the nick of time.

Fortunately, I'm the only resident and I spend the next four hours or so, (it feels like a week), calling for Hughie. When I'm not well and throwing up, at least calling for Hughie has a double meaning for me, my father was called Hughie but I'm feeling so rotten that I'm calling for the old man anyway.

After what seems like an eternity cuddling the 'Armitage' Shanks, I manage to stagger back to my dismal little room feeling totally sorry for myself and eventually drift off into a troubled sleep.

Day's statistics: 40.5 miles – Average speed – 10.5mph – Time taken – 3hours 50 minutes – Max speed – 35.5mph

Chapter 21

Day 18 – Midleton to Youghall (19 miles)

It seems as though I have only been asleep for a matter of minutes when I awake at 8am with a feeling that the bathroom might again be needed as a matter of urgency, I contemplate my options for the day.

The thought of fifty hard miles in the saddle does not appeal to me with the joys of spring, but the thought of staying another twenty-four hours in this dingy little room is also not in the least bit appealing either. If only this had been the Maguire's back in Portstewart or the Hamilton's in Donegal, then I would happily have stayed put for another day or so, but there is just no way I am going to stay in this depressing guest house in Midleton.

After a long hot shower, I still don't feel much better, but I'm determined to get out of Midleton and at least put a few more miles under my tyres. A quick look at the map shows the holiday town of Youghall about a two-hour cycle away might be a good option, as holiday towns are always a good bet for decent B& Bs.

Making my way down to the dining room for breakfast, for the first time on the trip the smell of the good old Irish fry doesn't give me a boost, in fact I'm almost forced to make a quick dash back up to the bathroom.

Well aware that it is essential to take in some nutrition and plenty of fluids if I am to attempt at least a few miles, I manage to force down a few spoonfuls of cornflakes, a cup of tea and a large glass of orange juice. Rejecting the offer of a full Irish breakfast for the first time, I'm forced to tell the landlady my predicament and she offers some advice:

'Sure, there a gud chemist just across the street and they'll fix ye up wi a bottle naw problem,' she says. My mum always seemed to have a bottle for everything when I was a child, so this rang a bell.

Taking her advice, I pop over to the chemist shop where the friendly pharmacist is very helpful. She provides me with some pills which she assures me will settle my stomach.

'I think you might have picked up a touch of mild food poisoning,' she says, after I had outlined my symptoms. Not altogether what I wanted to hear.

After popping a couple of pills, I load up the bike and set off again along the N25. Every turn of the pedals is a major effort and to make matters worse, I'm cycling into a strong easterly headwind. The only consolation being that at least there is a separate cycle track with an excellent surface making life just a little easier. This part of east Cork is very flat with quite uninspiring scenery, and as I cycle along, I yearn to be back amidst the hills and scenery of West Cork and Kerry, but with only about three days left to cycle I press on towards Youghal.

As the morning progresses, the wind slowly strengthens, as I cross the river Dissour. It's a titanic effort just to turn over the pedals in my debilitated state as the wind reaches almost gale force.

With just another hour's cycling before I reach Youghal it's taking a superhuman effort just to stay upright never mind maintain any sort of forward momentum, but the thought of some rest and a hot shower spurs me over the last couple of miles. Fortunately, the last mile or so into the town is downhill but even then, the wind is so fierce that I must keep turning over the pedals to keep up any sort of speed.

The views away to my right over the Blackwater Estuary are superb, with the wind is whipping the waves into a frenzy of froth-capped tops, but the vista is lost on me as I struggle to keep upright in the gusts.

Entering Youghall, I stop at the first B&B sign that catches my eye. The Attracta Guest house has vacancies and as I'm in no mood to spend an hour or so contrasting and comparing the various establishments in the town, I gladly accept a room without even asking the price. Securing the bike to a gate in the back yard, I am shown up to a very pleasant room on the second floor overlooking the harbour, where I promptly collapse on the bed without even a second glance at the view.

After a hot shower and an hour's rest, I begin to feel almost human again and walk down into the town centre. With a population of around 8,000, Youghal is a pretty little town sitting at the entrance to the river Blackwater, but its downside is that it has one of the worst traffic bottlenecks in Ireland. Vehicles arriving off the Rosslare Ferry heading to Cork and other destinations in the south-east and south-west of Ireland must travel through the town centre. (A year later after my trip, a new by-pass was built around the town of Youghal solving its traffic problems).

Today the traffic is at a standstill, made worse by a funeral party as it makes its way along the street towards the cemetery at the northern end of the town. As is normal in Ireland I stop to pay my respects along with the rest of the people on the street, bowing my head as the hearse passes.

When the funeral party has passed, I stop at the tourist office to read some of the leaflets posted in the window. I'm aware that Youghal was the location for John Huston's famous film Moby Dick made in 1954 and based on the classic book of the same name written by Herman Melville written in 1851. My education was further enhanced though, when I read that it was also the home of Sir Walter Raleigh. On his estate just outside the town at Myrtle Grove, he planted the first potatoes in Europe in 1596, at least we have Sir Walter to thank for providing us with our staple diet.

I'm amused to read that in 1610 Youghal town council was so concerned about.

> *'divers lewd persons deflowering virgins that such persons will be fined for the offence ranging from £40, if the girl was the daughter of an alderman, down to £5 if she was the daughter of a groom'*

An early illustration of the class system if ever I saw one.

During the 14th Century, this small harbour town traded extensively in wines, spirits, spices, and salt with ports all over Europe, but the trade declined when steam replaced sail during the 1860s and tides gradually built up a dangerous sand bar across the harbour mouth.

Still feeling a bit queasy since leaving Midleton I once again by-pass all the pubs with Guinness signs, and although not in the least bit hungry, I take a seat in a homely looking restaurant. Having not eaten solids for forty-eight hours, I need to get some food inside me if I'm to make a decent fist of tomorrow's cycle. I order an omelette and force it down.

I'm back at the Attracta by 8pm and ready to settle down for the night, hoping that I will have recovered enough for an assault on the fifty or so miles to Tramore, my target for tomorrow. The stomach bug has left me seriously weakened, and my whole-body aches when I make my usual evening phone call to my wife. When I tell her that I am considering packing it in tomorrow and get a train up to Dublin, there is lengthy pause before she responds:

> *'You will not, you've done 80 percent of the trip and there is no way you're packing it in now. Why don't you rest up for a day or two and see how you feel?'*

She is adamant that I should not give up and that I should try and get a good night's rest and hope that I will be feeling better in the morning. Closing my eyes at the end of day eighteen and with Liz's words ringing in my ears, I'm determined to finish the challenge of cycling around my home country.

Day's statistics: 19.1 miles – Average speed – 7.8mph – Time taken – 2hours 27 minutes – Max speed – 16.1mph

Chapter 22

Day 19 – Youghall to Tramore (47 miles)

Day nineteen, and I awake feeling a good deal better that I did yesterday. Making my way to the dining room I'm looking forward to a full Irish breakfast again for the first time in two days.

Chatting to a lovely old Irish lady and her son over breakfast, she tells me, 'Sure, he's a wonderful man, and you wouldn't think he was priest,' she says in the way that proud mothers do – to her offspring's intense embarrassment.

As he's not wearing a priest's uniform, I would have had no way of knowing that he was a priest until she tells me. She is a lovely old lady and very proud of her son who is serving the Catholic Church over in Boston, USA.

They are both impressed with my marathon cycle trip.

'Maybe your next one will across the US?' her son says.

'Perhaps another time,' I respond, aware that it's at least three times the distance of my Ireland trip.

With another day's hard cycling ahead, I gaze out from my bedroom window across the harbour. Yesterday's high winds have still not abated and are whipping the tops off the waves in showers of white foam, but at least it's not raining, and my stomach is functioning somewhere near to its normal state.

A mile or so out of Youghal I cross the Tourig River and into the fifteenth county of my trip – Waterford. It's easy to see from this point on the bay why Youghal is such a good natural harbour, its entrance is quite narrow but quickly opens out to provide a safe and sheltered anchorage. Even with a north easterly blowing at somewhere near gale force the yachts moored in the harbour are riding comfortably on their moorings.

I cross the river Blackwater and head on along the N25 through the small village of Kinsalebeg. The road goes up and down like a roller coaster for the next five or six miles as I cycle on through the villages of Grange and Kiely's Cross, and then on through the beautifully wooded hillsides of the Drum Hills. At the top of a steep hill, I stop briefly to admire the excellent views across Dungarvan Bay, before plunging headlong down the R911 towards Dungarvan town.

Stopping for a drink and a breather at the harbour, which is always a good place for a rest in Irish coastal towns, I consult my guidebook. With a population of just over 7,000, Dungarvan, the administrative centre of County Waterford, sits at the sunken end of a long limestone trough. The town was named after St Garvan who founded a monastery nearby in the seventh century and is the birthplace of Ernest Walton, whose work on nuclear fission won him the Nobel Prize for physics in 1951.

Fifteen or so miles inland from Dungarvan lie the Knockmealdown Mountains, more a range of hills really, as the highest summit rises to a mere 1,000 feet. I mention this, because the village of Lismore in the foothills of the mountains is home to one of Ireland's most famous authors on cycling, Dervla Murphy, whom I paid tribute to at the beginning of the book. It's tempting to take a detour inland and perhaps have a chat with the great lady, but with my still slightly delicate stomach and an overwhelming desire to reach Dublin as soon as possible, I decide otherwise and head on out of the town over the Barnawee Bridge on the coastal R675 east towards Waterford.

The R675 twists, turns, and undulates, as I make my way over the River Dalligan before turning onto the Stradbally More Road and on towards the village of Stradbally itself. At Stradbally Cove I cross a bridge over the river Tay. I do as double take and wonder whether I'm actually in Scotland, but there really is a River Tay in this part of Waterford.

At Stradbally I turn onto an even narrower road through Knockrour and down to Ballyvooney Cover where I cross another bridge. Twenty minutes of cycling along this beautiful coastline, I re-join the R675 again at Bunmahon where it winds its way directly east.

After a mile or so, a large sign catches my eye; 'Welcome to the Copper Coast'. Stopping for a drink and a snack, a plaque affixed to a wall informs me that copper was been extensively mined along this section of the coast during the later eighteenth and early nineteenth centuries. At this very point, two Cornish engine houses once stood, one lifting iron ore from depths of almost a quarter of a mile, whilst the other pumped seawater out, before closing in 1850 when the ore supplies ran out.

The Copper Coast is now a Unesco Geopark extending for some ten miles from Kilfarrasy in the east to Stradbally in the west. The first Geopark designated on the island of Ireland, its rocks and geosites tell the story of undersea volcanos, arid deserts, and dramatic ice-ages while its human history is inextricably linked with its landscape from ancient to early modern times. After this brief educational stop, I set off again through the villages of Kilmurrin towards Tramore, my target for the day.

The effects of the stomach bug have gone by now, and with the sun on my back I cycle along this spectacular and scenic coastline in high spirits and at peace with the world. The cliffs to my right drop vertically down to small shingly inlets, reminding me very much of the north Devon coastline with its rocky promontories and small harbour villages tucked neatly away under jagged rock faces.

My guidebook gives this part of the coast the accolade as 'the best coastal scenery in Ireland' but I may just be a tad biased though if I dispute this claim, as in my opinion the Antrim coast might just have a bit of a claim to that title?

The R675 turns inland again at Annestown and half an hour later I arrive at Tramore. This small seaside town is one of Ireland's premier seaside resorts, and as it is still a few weeks before the busy holiday season, I should have no difficulty in finding a B&B. On the Waterford Road every other house has a B&B sign hanging outside, all displaying vacancies. Spoilt for choice, I opt for the Asgard House, the nearest one to the centre of town.

From my room in the Asgard, I get an excellent view down to the beach and across the bay towards Brownstown Head (that is if I stand on a chair, stick my head out the window and swivel it at ninety degrees).

On a practical front, one of the issues I face daily is washing and drying my clothes. Arriving at my B&Bs late each day, it is difficult to get my small amount of clothes dry ready for the following day's cycle. With the rain over the past couple of days, my things are still very damp when I arrive in Tramore. I'll leave you to ponder on the smells emanating from my saddlebags. I've worked out that the easiest way to wash my clothes is to take them into the shower with me, or to use the wash hand basin in my room – thank heavens for 'wash and go'. Fortunately, the weather today in Tramore is fine and I'm able to hang my clothes out of the bedroom window to dry.

Tramore is a delightful little seaside town with a lovely bay encircled by three miles of golden sandy beaches. It has attracted holidaymakers since Georgian times, particularly wealthy Dubliners anxious to get away from the hustle, bustle, and grime of the city.

The huge expanse of wide sandy beach over a mile long, is used for the Tramore Horse Races three times a year. People flock from all over Ireland to enjoy the excitement of the races.

Abstaining from Tramore's amusement arcades, and for the second evening running, I pass on the Guinness, and settle instead for an excellent light meal in a spotless little café up in the old part of the town followed by another early night.

Day's statistics: 47.3 miles – Average speed – 7.8mph – Time taken – 6hours 00 minutes – Max speed – 30.6mph

Chapter 23

Day 20 – Tramore to Curracloe (44 miles)

Day twenty dawns bright and blustery and, with my stomach just about back to something like normal, I study my map over a hearty Irish breakfast in the Asgard. The town of Wexford, about a fifty-mile cycle, looks like a good option for my next overnight stop.

Following my plan of trying to avoid major towns and cities, I decide to cycle via Passage East where there is a ferry across the Barrow Estuary to Ballyhack, thereby avoiding Waterford.

Leaving Tramore I set off along the R675 before joining the R685 a mile or so out of the town towards Passage East. Cycling along, I pass through the village of Woodstown where the wide expanse of the Waterford estuary opens up glistening in the morning sunshine. The rivers Barrow, Nore and Suir all pour into this estuary before making their way 'hand in hand' into the Celtic Sea.

Stopping briefly to admire the view towards the Hook Head peninsula where it curves gracefully into St Georges Channel just beyond Creadan Head, I look back across the estuary to the low-lying Hook Head Lighthouse with its twin black bands. This old lighthouse has always been of great significant to sailors as it marked the beginning of the vital shipping route into Waterford harbour. The oldest lighthouse in Europe dating back to 1172, it has been a unique landmark for locals and visitors to this corner of Wexford for generations. Prior to its erection in 1172 there was a beacon on the headland since the 5th Century.

Following the western shore of the estuary, I cycle on through the hamlet of Crooke and a few minutes later I'm coasting down a steep hill into Passage East. As the ferry has just departed for its 10-minute crossing over the river Suir to Ballyhack, I take the opportunity to rest my legs awhile, take in the scenery and consult my guidebook once again.

It was here at Passage East where, in 1171, Henry II landed with 4,000 men and 400 ships when he invaded Ireland. Richard II is also thought to have landed at the same spot with 34,000 troops in June 1399.

This is scheduled to be my fifth and last ferry crossing of the trip, a crossing that will save me around thirty miles of hard cycling avoiding Waterford town.

Cycling ashore at Ballyhack, I enter my sixteenth county – Wexford. Have I really cycled through fifteen counties and covered nearly 900 miles over the last twenty days or is it just all a dream?

The first half a mile or so out of the Ballyhack ferry terminal is on a flat section of the R770, but on reaching Arthurstown and joining the R733 the road begins to rise steeply again. In the top three of climbs I have encountered on the trip so far, I ignore the pain and the desire to get off and walk, drop down into my lowest gear, put my brain into neutral and sweat on uphill towards the village of Ramsgrange.

It's a relief when the steep hills soon turn into no more than little tiddlers, and I am cruising along towards Wellingtonbridge, over the river Corock and on through Waddington and Hilltown towards Wexford.

Approaching the town, the traffic begins to increase and once again I use my well-practised cycling skills to avoid ending up in the gutter with the various forms of dead wildlife. B&Bs seem thin on the ground as I cycle into Wexford, so I pedal on down through the suburb of Rocks Lane and into the centre. Once again, the tourist office seems to be my best bet and the assistant tells me with the usual Irish charm that:

'There are plenty of B&Bs on the outskirts of the town, but if you want to stay somewhere quieter try Curracloe just a few miles up the coast, it's lovely spot.' (What she omits to inform me is that Curracloe has no B & Bs as I'm soon to find out). As it's a pleasant afternoon and still only 4pm, I decide to browse around Wexford before taking her advice and heading up towards Curracloe.

Opposite the tourist office, a huge 10-foot-high bronze statue on the other side of the road catches my eye, so I wander across to investigate. The plaque underneath it tells me that it is of Commodore John Barry, United States Navy. Barry was born on 17 March 1745 (St Patrick's day) in the small village of Ballysampson some eight miles south of Wexford. When Barry's family were evicted from their home by their British landlord, they moved to Rosslare on the coast where his uncle worked a fishing skiff. At that point he was determined upon a life as a seaman. At the age of 15 Barry's family joined the hordes of emigrants for the 'Promised Land' across the Atlantic. The Barry family settled in Philadelphia where he joined the US Navy, quickly rising to the rank of commander. At the age of thirty-one, he took command of the *Lexington* when it captured the first naval vessel ever taken by an American man o' war.

The United States of America, in recognition of his outstanding contribution to the naval history of his adopted country, presented this bronze statue to the people of Wexford in 1805.

Gazing out over Wexford's quiet harbour it is hard to imagine that this very spot was buzzing with excitement over 200 years ago, when the first ever steam-powered ship chugged its way out of the port on its inaugural crossing of the Irish Sea to London.

Having found out just a little about Wexford's history, I remount and cross the Wexford bridge over the River Slaney and wearily make my way the last six miles of the day up towards Curracloe.

With a population of just under 600, Curracloe is made up of a shop, a hotel and a pub surrounded by a cluster of houses. A quick tour does not reveal even one B&B sign. The only accommodation seems to be the very swish modern looking Curracloe motel. My mind drifts back to the same scenario when I cycled into Maam Cross on day ten. Short of cycling the six miles back into Wexford, I'm left with little choice and with only two more nights left, I throw almost all the remainder of budget out of the window and book a room.

The Curracloe Motel is truly a luxury, a huge double bed, a Jacuzzi bath that could have accommodated me, my bike and all my worldly possessions along with the biggest TV I have seen on the trip greets me.

Totally rejuvenated after a half an hour in the foaming tub, I browse through the leaflets I picked up in reception. One in particular catches my eye, '*The Saving of Private Ryan'* puts Curracloe on the map. Ballinesker Beach on Curracloe Strand was used for the filming of the D-Day sequence in Saving Private Ryan, due to its similarity to Omaha Beach in Normandy. 'Filming began on 27 June 1997 and lasted for two months,' it reads.

Steven Spielberg the director had scoured the world looking for a beach as near as possible to replicate the Normandy beaches and discovered that this little 8-mile stretch of beach in SW Ireland was perfect for the job. Apparently at that time Curracloe lacked 3-phase electricity, but when the film company decided to film there, it was installed.

Although the motel has a comfortable bar and restaurant, I follow my usual pattern and walk the couple of hundred yards up to the solitary pub in the village, Furlongs Lounge Bar, or the Curracloe Roadhouse (it seems to have two names for some reason). Standing at the bar for the obligatory two and half minutes waiting for my pint (yes, I've now got my appetite for the black stuff back), I glance around rather the scruffy and noisy lounge. There is an empty table near the door and as I sit down, a framed newspaper article hung on the wall above my head catches my eye.

'The bar that Tom Hanks Missed' proclaims the headline. The article goes on to say that during filming of Saving of Private Ryan, leading star Tom Hanks never once set foot in the Furlong Bar during the many weeks he was in the village.

As there is no sign of any food being available in Furlongs Bar, the aroma emanating from Nellies takeaway in the car park at the rear of the pub gets me salivating, but with my stomach still a tad fragile, I opt for an omelette back at the Motel.

With days flying past, I'm not sure which day of the week it, but a poster in the lounge reminds me that it is Friday. 'Friday night is ceilidh night' it announces. Tempting as it is to take in the ceilidh, I resist the temptation. A late night coupled with the obligatory six pints of Guinness will probably spell disaster tomorrow, so I head for bed at 9.30pm where I curl up under the fresh clean sheets and nod off almost immediately.

My dreams are rudely interrupted when I'm awakened by what sounds like a herd of wildebeests pounding through the room below. Unfortunately, my room happens to be right above the function room where the ceilidh is now in full swing.

Putting a pillow over my head I try to ignore the heavy beat of the music, but it's so loud that the floor is vibrating, and I can hear every word of the songs being blasted out by the DJ.

Getting back to sleep is impossible, so I consider my options: I can get dressed again and join the ceilidh, I can read or watch TV and wait until it finishes, or I can go downstairs and ask to be moved to a quieter room. I'm quite tempted to go down and join the party as nothing beats a good Irish ceilidh, but I'm aware that the temptations of the Guinness will be difficult to resist and that I have my penultimate days cycling ahead tomorrow. The memories of the 'morning after' in Carnlough are still fresh in my mind, so that option is out. If I read or watch TV then I could still be awake at two or three in the morning - this is Ireland after all, and no ceilidh finishes before that sort of time. My only option is to ask for a quieter room, so I throw on my tracksuit and pop down to reception where the duty manager is most understanding when I explain my predicament.

'Not a problem sur, we'll have you moved to a quieter room. We don't usually get guests going to bed at 9.30pm on a Friday night,' he says with a wry smile.

It's a bit of a nuisance repacking my panniers and moving to another room, but although I can still just hear music, I soon drift off into a deep sleep.

Day's statistics: 44.00 miles – Average speed – 8.9mph – Time taken – 4hours 55 minutes – Max speed – 29.00mph

Chapter 24

Day 21 Curracloe to Arklow (38 miles)

Considering how difficult it was to get sleep last night, I awake early and am the first person down to breakfast – perhaps the ceilidh has taken its toll on the other residents?

Leaving the Curracloe Motel I take the R743 towards the beach where the Saving Private Ryan scenes were filmed. Pausing for a few minutes to look along this glorious stretch of sandy beach, I try to envisage what the scene might have looked like during the filming, and at once it becomes obvious why this beach was ideal. As there are very few modern houses along the skyline, from the sea the low sweeping dunes must have looked very much like those of the Normandy beaches where the real D-Day landings took place on 6 June 1944. The land above the Normandy beaches has now been built upon so much that it would have been difficult to obtain any sense of authenticity if they had been used for the film.

Setting off again I pass a holiday village where one of the actual landing craft made for the film still stands, providing the local children with an ideal playhouse. With my curiosity satisfied I pedal on, joining the R742 up the coast towards Arklow.

At the village of Gorey, I join the R772 and am soon entering Wicklow, my seventeenth county. It's a great feeling passing under a big sign that says, 'Welcome to Wicklow – the end is in sight.' (it didn't actually say that, I made it up.)

Fifteen minutes later and I'm entering Arklow. Negotiating the rush hour traffic through the town is quite daunting, as cars and vans inch their way up the main street. The last thing I wanted after a hard day in the saddle was my mind wandering and ending up in A&E, so I kept my wits about me.

For many years the town of Arklow was one of Ireland's most important east coast trading ports and shipbuilding town. During the eighteenth century, hundreds of ships were coming and going on a regular basis from its neat little harbour bound for Britain and continental Europe. Sailing ships and wooden-hulled fishing boats were built in Arklow's Tyrell Yard – Sir Francis Chichester's Gypsy Moth 3 was built here in 1958.

With thirty-eight miles under my tyres since leaving Curracloe and fatigue setting in, I decide that Arklow will be my last overnight stop, leaving me just over fifty miles left to cycle to reach Dublin port tomorrow.

Cycling down the main street I keep my eyes open for a B&B, but as they seem scarce, I head towards the Avoca River. Glancing down to my right along the south Quay just before the bridge, a B&B sign on a large grey house overlooking the harbour catches my eye, so I decide to check it out for my overnight stop.

The Weimar B&B has a room available and after checking in, the hosts invite me for a cup of tea in the lounge.

'Are you on a cycling holiday?' says landlord Tim as I collapse into a comfy chair.

'I'm just finishing a cycle ride round Ireland, and this is my final stop before Dublin. I've been on the road for twenty days,' I reply nonchalantly as though it's something one does every week.

'That's some effort, Cecil, where do you come from?

'I'm from Stockport just south of Manchester, do you know it?'

'I certainly do, my brother lives there, and we go over regularly for a bit of golf.'

'Where does he play Tim? I play a bit of golf myself.'

'He is a member at Reddish Vale, lovely course but a bit hard on the old legs. Do you know it?'

By now I'm beginning to realise that this conversation could be interesting.

'That's my club as well, what's his name?'

'It's Paddy, same surname, Weadick?'

I nearly fall off my chair as Paddy just happens to be one of my golfing buddies and my son was in the same class in school as Paddy's two children. By pure chance in Arklow, I knock on the door of my friend Paddy Weadick's brother's B&B – what an unbelievable coincidence.

After a good old chat with Tim, it's early evening when I walk the few hundred yards from the Weimar up into the centre of Arklow town for what is probably going to me my last evening meal of the trip. The bars and restaurants are buzzing with activity, and I'm spoiled for choice. I'm tempted to treat myself to a sumptuous banquet in a posh restaurant, but for some reason, the smells emanating from a takeaway van near to the river lures me. Chicken and chips 'al fresco' is to be my celebratory 'last evening' meal.

It's a beautiful summer evening as I sit on a bench in Arklow, watching the River Avoca wind its way towards the sea contentedly munching my chicken and chips. With only one more day's cycling to go, it's time for contemplation. The last three weeks have flown past in a blur of exhaustion, excitement, and nostalgia, but I'm now ready to get home to see my wife and family again.

A tear rolls down my cheek, dripping onto my chips, as it dawns on me that I am on the verge of achieving my ambition to cycle alone round Ireland.

Day's statistics: 38.00 miles – Average speed – 9.3mph – Time taken – 4hours 03 minutes – Max speed – 27.6mph

Chapter 25

Day 22 – Arklow to Dublin (53 miles)

It's a Sunday morning when the Weadick's wave me off from Arklow on the final day on my cycle round Ireland. My spirits are high as I cycle over the Nineteen Arches Bridge, the longest handmade stone bridge in Ireland, and along the R750 coast road northwards.

After half an hour of easy cycling I pass through the village of Ardanary where I can just make out in the distance away to my right the promontory of Mizen Head jutting out into the Irish Sea. A few minutes later and I'm passing the curving sandy beach of Brittas Bay and then on through Three Mile Water and Dunbur towards Wicklow.

A county of contrasts, Wicklow has it all – wild moorland, green valleys, red squirrels, sandy beaches, and a multitude of large country houses. In 1835 the county experienced a real wild-west style gold rush, when gold was discovered in the beds of the rivers which descend from the summit of the mountains. Many thousands of people descended on the area to try and find their fortune at that time - most without success.

Due to some generous tax incentives, grants from the Irish Government and its spectacular scenery, a host of blockbuster films have been shot on location in various parts of Wicklow. Films such as Braveheart, Zardoz, Kidnapped, My Left Foot, Henry V and countless other hits were made in and around the Wicklow Mountains. Disney even constructed an entire castle in the Glendasan Valley Lead Mines to film the Reign of Fire, and the classic series *Ballykissangel* was filmed on location in the town of Avoca, some five or six miles inland from Arklow.

With only about a couple of hours cycling left, I pedal furiously towards Wicklow town. At Rathnew Old Village, the R750 becomes the R761, and I head on northwards towards Dublin. Away to me left the Wicklow mountains rise majestically and I'm taken back once again to my childhood in the 1950s when my parents brought me here for a holiday.

With the end now in sight, I put my head down over the handlebars and cycle furiously through the villages of Kilcoole and Newcastle before arriving at Greystones.

With Dublin looming, I don't tarry in Greystones and cycle on five miles into Bray, or the 'Brighton of Ireland' as it is commonly called, where I stop for a snack and a drink and consult my guidebook.

Until the middle of the nineteenth century Bray was a dowdy little fishing village, but it is now one of Ireland's leading holiday resorts. Within a half an hour from Dublin at the southern end of the DART Line, it's great circular sweep of sandy beaches stretches away to my right up towards Killiney, a beautiful bay that was known in Victorian times as Ireland's Bay of Naples.

Soon after leaving Bray, I cross the bridge over the river Dargle, join the R119 and into the eighteenth and final county of my trip – Dublin.

Cycling on through the leafy lanes of affluent Killiney I stop for few minutes to gaze down over Dun Laoghaire harbour from where I set off twenty days ago before dropping down into Dalkey.

Three hundred yards off the coast at this point lies Dalkey Island. During the 18th Century it was called 'The Kingdom of Dalkey Island' with its own monarch the King of Dalkey, Emperor of the Muglins, defender of his own faith and respecter of all others and Sovereign of the Illustrious Order of the Lobster and Periwinkle.

A spoilsport government of the time however banned such paganism, but rumour has it that the ceremony is still carried out each year by a group of locals behind closed doors.

Passing the Forty Foot leap at Sandycove near the Martello Tower, I glance down to an open-air swimming pool and beach, apparently the only legal nudist beach in Ireland - no sign of any nudists today though as the beach is deserted.

A few minutes later I stop for a few minutes at the Ferry Port of Dun Laoghaire from where I started my journey three weeks ago. The last three weeks have just flown past, and it seems like only yesterday when I cycled

down the ramp from the ferry sitting in the harbour onto Irish soil, yet it also seems like a lifetime ago. Glancing across to the harbour, I shed a tear.

My ferry home today departs from Dublin port meaning that I have another eight miles left to cycle.

I'm now once again cycling along the N31 that hugs the south side of Dublin Bay with the DART (Dublin Area Rapid Transport) running alongside and the views across the Bay to the north are as superb as they were three weeks ago.

A mile or so out of Dun Laoghaire a large sign beams down on me 'Baile Atha Cliath Welcome to Dublin.' For the first time in twenty-two days, I lift both hands from the handlebars, raise them above my head in a Tour de France salute and punch the sky in a fit of sheer exuberance.

'Yes! I did it', I shout at the top of my voice oblivious to the stares of the passers-by.

With 1,000 miles and twenty-two days behind me, the sense of achievement feels immense – I have circumnavigated the Island of Ireland using my own pedal power.

Day's statistics: 53.1 miles – Average speed – 9.3mph – Time taken – 5hours 42 minutes – Max speed – 29.

EPILOGUE

The beauty of the Irish landscape lies in the never-ending change in colour. A momentary break of sun transforms the sky from dull yellow to bright, rain-washed blue. It lights a hillside to brilliant green, or mottles it a brown or green mauve. A moment later it disappears, dashing the sky back again to mournful purples and misty greys. So it is with the Irish character. What is too harshly called the 'superstition' of Irish folklore coexists with Catholic piety; a puritanical morality goes hand in hand with the hilarity of a race meeting. The loyalty too harshly named 'clannishness' runs side by side with the personal acquisitiveness of a peasant proprietorship. Small wonder then the Irish feel no foreigner will ever fully understand'.

Conrad Arensberg. The Irish Countryman 1937

Cycling around the country of birth gave me the opportunity to taste, touch, smell, and talk to the real Ireland – the Ireland Arensberg referred to in 1937.

I feasted my eyes on the beauty of Ireland's wonderful countryside and coastline, with its wild mosaic landscape of never-ending changes of colours. I tasted the freshness of the air, the wonderful food and of course the black stuff.

I touched the hands of many Irish people. The land, with its green grass, flowers, rocks, and rivers. I smelt the many and varied odours, baking bread over an open peat fire, the unforgettable smell of a real Irish pub and the smells from the famous distilleries of Bushmills and Jamesons. Freshly caught mussels, and of course the unforgettable smell of a fresh Irish summer evening after a heavy shower of rain. I talked to genuine Irish folk whose families have lived in the country for centuries.

There is more to Ireland than simply the wonderful scenery - which though sometimes harsh, is rarely boring: the wonder that is the Giant's Causeway, the beauty of Killarney's Lakes and the raw splendour of the Aran Islands are only but a few of the best-known attractions of a country that has now firmly embraced the 21st Century. Yet rounding the next bend I was often transported back to an old world trapped in time, to an historic romantic Ireland, an Ireland that clung to Christian tradition and learning when the rest of Europe was a pagan barbaric place.

The Island of Ireland was not always the happy place to live as it is now. It has survived many invaders who tried in vain for centuries to take over the land and to crush the spirit of a passionate and patriotic people, but the Irish have emerged stronger and more resilient that ever. The country has changed from being one of emigration to one of immigration, as many prodigal sons return to their roots.

I was well aware of the reputation the Irish have for the vernacular and in particular for their willingness to 'talk you to death.' Everyone has a story to tell me, a joke to share or a song to sing, and in most cases with the most beautiful voice. Every pub I visited had its own 'professional' genealogist who knows everything about everyone in the town and who was only too willing to tell you the family history of some poor soul over a pint of the black stuff.

'D'ye see Paddy the smuggler over there?' one indicated with his thumb towards a man sitting on a stool at the end of the bar.

'What?' I ask, 'You mean he smuggles for a living?'

'Shure his granfather was hanged for smuggling.'

I find it hard not to laugh but it is said in all seriousness as family history is often passed down from generation to generation. I met many typical Irish people, you know the type, a dreamy sort, only interested in music, singing and, of course, the black stuff. The sort you could happily spend a wet evening in the pub with; they are a lot brighter than they make out. They act like a fifteen-year-old although well into their fifties, but behind those twinkling eyes their grandparent's rigid Catholic value systems are well established.

There is something about the air in Ireland that induces a sense of calm and comfort, and as I made my way round the island, I began to appreciate the true value of life. Ireland is one of those places where you can never be alone, but whilst I was on my own as I cycled each day, I never felt lonely – people waved to me as I passed them by and whenever I stopped the conversation flowed, mainly about my crazy trip but often about the weather, the price of whisky or even politics.

In Ireland don't expect to go into a pub for a quiet drink, the locals expect you to stay until the landlord literally kicks you out on the street, as I found out in Carnlough.

I spent hours in blissful solitude on empty, isolated lanes with 'grand' (to use an Irish expression) views. Then there was the madness of dodging rush-hour traffic in small towns and villages and trying to follow the road signs in a system that seems to be designed to prevent visitors finding their way to their destination. Perhaps they want you to stop a local and ask for directions? If so, you will be there for at least ten minutes whilst Paddy gives you the history of the area, and you'll usually end up having a pint with him in the nearest pub. Many signposts in Ireland seem to have a finger missing and the one I wanted was always the one that was missing.

It gave me immense satisfaction to cycle through seventeen counties and the four proud provinces of the twentieth largest island in the world in twenty-one days. When people asked me where my back up and support was, I would point to the bike and say, 'this is all the support I need'. They would wander off shaking their heads or offer to buy me a pint. Speaking of pints, if I had accepted all the pints I was offered during the trip, I would probably still be lying in some ditch in County Kerry.

Some years ago, I came across a small verse amongst my mother's possessions and for me it sums up Ireland. I apologise to the author who I'm unable to trace, but I'm sure he or she will not mind my using it to conclude this book.

Erratum

I actually made this trip in June 2001 not June 2002 as published in error.

Contrary to what I write on page 1, whilst the Euro had been adopted by Ireland at that time, the Irish pound or Punt as it was known, was still legal tender until February 2002 – apologies.

Sure a little bit of heaven
Fell from out the sky one day,
And it settled on the Ocean
In a spot so far away.
And when Angels saw it
Why, it looked so sweet and fair
They said 'Suppose we leave it as it look so peaceful there.'
So they sprinkled it with stardust
Just to make the Shamrock grow,
It's the only place you'll find it
No matter where you go.
And they sprinkled it with silver
Just to make the lakes look grand.
And when they had it finished
Why they called it IRELAND.